Effective Director

Published by:
Lotus Press : Publishers & Distributors

Effective Director

Kiran Kaushik

Lotus PRESS

4735/22, Prakash Deep Building
Ansari Road, Darya Ganj,
New Delhi-110002

Lotus Press : Publishers & Distributors
Unit No. 220, 2nd Floor, 4735/22, Prakash Deep Building,
Ansari Road, Darya Ganj, New Delhi- 110002
Ph.: 32903912, 23280047 • E-mail : lotus_press@sify.com
www.lotuspress.co.in

Effective Director

ISBN: 978-81-8382-281-7

Published by : **Lotus Press : Publishers & Distributors** New Delhi-110002
Printed at : Concept Imprint, Delhi

PREFACE

Being an effective director is a learned, not innate, skill. Nor is it a static proposition. Standards for directors change over time, especially as we consider more about what directors should do, and as we learn what happens when there are important things they don't do. To ensure and improve their effectiveness, directors must continually evaluate how best to meet their fiduciary, legal, ethical and corporate governance responsibilities. To help in this undertaking, this is the first of an occasional series of "how to" columns on directing.

The duties and responsibilities of directors for the effective governance of their companies have never been greater. The success of every company depends ultimately on the calibre of its directors and the effectiveness of its board. In fulfilling the role of an effective director, an individual must take a proactive approach, going beyond the minimum legal obligations

This book shows how directors can add real value to their organisations and, in the process, gain a strong sense of satisfaction from their roles. It would be valuable for all directors—whether of public or private companies or those filling equivalent roles in not-for-profit organizations. It should be especially helpful to all those who are seeking to improve performance or who are seeking to take on the role in new organizations.

Kiran Kaushik

CONTENTS

1

WHO IS AN EFFECTIVE DIRECTOR?

WHAT IS A DIRECTOR?

A company as an artificial legal entity can act only through its human 'agents', i.e. its directors or officers. Although in many private companies the shareholders and directors are the same people, in their capacities as directors they are the legally accountable custodians of the company who may be liable for penalties if they do not ensure the company's compliance with its legal obligations.

A director is any person occupying the position of director or alternate director of a company, by whatever name he may be designated. The term 'board' is the collective term used to designate the directors when they act together as a group.'

Legally, there is of course no distinction between executive and non-executive directors, nor indeed between directors and officers of the company, and they all remain equally accountable for the proper conduct of its affairs. There are in fact no such creatures in law as executive and non-executive directors, and they, along with the independent and shadow directors are little more than creations of corporate governance literature. A director, once appointed is just that—a director of the company.

Executive directors are simply directors who have certain executive responsibilities, which are distinct from and in addition to their role as directors of the company. The term 'officer' is often used interchangeably with director but it specifically includes a chief executive manager.

The directors of an organization are the persons who are members of its board. Several specific terms categorize directors by the presence or absence of their other relationships to the organization. An inside director is a director who is also an employee, officer, major shareholder, or someone similarly connected to the organization. Inside directors represent the interests of the entity's stakeholders, and often have special knowledge of its inner workings, its financial or market position, and so on.

Typical inside directors are:

- A Chief Executive Officer (CEO) who may also be Chairman of the Board.
- Other executives of the organization, such as its Chief Financial Officer (CFO) or Executive Vice President.
- Large shareholders (who may or may not also be employees or officers).
- Representatives of other stakeholders such as labour unions, major lenders, or members of the community in which the organization is located.

The role and responsibilities of a board of directors vary depending on the nature and type of business entity and the laws applying to the entity. For example, the nature of the business entity may be one that is traded on a public market (public company), not traded on a public market (a private, limited or closely held company), owned by family members (a family business), or exempt from income taxes (a non-profit, not for profit, or tax-exempt entity). There are numerous types of business entities available throughout the world such as a corporation, limited liability company, cooperative, business trust, partnership, private limited company, and public limited company.

Much of what has been written about boards of directors relates to boards of directors of business entities actively traded on public markets. More recently, however, material is becoming available for boards of private and closely held businesses including family businesses.

APPOINTMENT OF DIRECTORS

Although the company's shareholders are usually authorized by the articles to appoint directors, in practice the board of directors appoints most directors. These appointments must then be confirmed at the first Annual General Meeting (AGM) after their appointment.

In manay companies, on appointment, directors must sign a Consent to Act as director within 28 days. Non-compliance does not invalidate the appointment, but is an offence under the law. Some companies require directors to hold qualification shares to qualify their appointment as directors. Where this is a provision in the articles, the shares must be taken up within two months of appointment.

Alternate Directors

Directors can, with the approval of the board, appoint alternate directors. Alternates act on behalf of directors when directors cannot personally fulfil their duties.

When serving in an alternate capacity, alternate directors have the same rights, duties and responsibilities as any other director and there is no distinction drawn in law between principal and alternate directors. The termination of the appointment of the principal director will ipso facto terminate the appointment of the alternate director.

Service Agreements

In addition to the statutory requirements above, many executive directors also enter into a fixed term service agreement with their companies, that further regulates their relationship with the organization. King II recommends that the term of these contracts should not exceed three years.

Induction and Training

Directors undergo a company induction when joining the board of a company. It also recommends training for directors with no prior board experience, and ongoing training as changing circumstances warrant.

Training should be formal and should include an overview of the business of the company and the legal responsibilities of a director covering at least the following:

- company law as it applies to directors
- the roles and responsibilities of directors
- duties and liabilities of directors
- financial interpretation of company accounts, and
- an awareness of non-financial matters relevant to the company

Persons Disqualified from Being a Director

The following persons cannot be directors:

— a body corporate

— a minor or person with no legal capacity (e.g. due to mental illness)

— any person whom the Court has ordered cannot be a director or officer

The following persons cannot be directors unless authorized by the Court:

— an un-rehabilitated insolvent

— any person removed from an office of trust because of misconduct, and

— any person convicted of offences such as theft, fraud, forgery, uttering, perjury, corruption or dishonesty in connection with the formation or management of a company.

The standard articles of association also imposes restrictions on the persons who may be appointed as directors. A director must resign if he:

— is no longer capable of being a director in terms of of the Companies Act

— without the consent of the company in a general meeting, holds any other office of profit under the company except that of chief executive or manager

— is absent without permission of the board for more than six months from meetings of directors held during that period

— is directly or indirectly interested in any contract or proposed contract with the company and fails to declare this interest and the nature thereof in the manner required by law

Disqualification

Directorships end if the director becomes disqualified to act as a director for any of the reasons set out above.

Removal

The shareholders of a company who follow the procedure laid down by national company law can also remove directors. Removal takes place even if the director has a service contract, although depending on the circumstances of the removal, the company may be liable to pay compensation to a director who has been removed from office. Some companies amend their articles to allow the board to remove directors from office, however the standard articles do not contain this provision.

Retirement

Most articles of association require a third of the board to retire by rotation at each AGM. These directors are usually reappointed but need not be, thus giving members the opportunity to accept the retirement of directors they are not satisfied with.

Resignation

Directors may resign by tendering a letter of resignation. A director may resign for personal reasons, to resolve a conflict of interests, at the request of the chairman or because of the company's insolvency (in which case the director should seek professional advice).

DUTIES OF DIRECTORS

Directors' duties arise from the following sources:

- the common law
- statutes
- the memorandum and articles of association of the company
- service agreements specifically entered between the director and the company

— resolutions passed at members' or directors' meetings
— the rules of a regulatory body, if any

Common Law Duties

A Director's Fiduciary Duty

'Every director is bound at common law by a separate and distinct fiduciary duty to the company (the term 'fiduciary' being derived from the Latin 'fiduciarius' meaning 'of trust'). Directors owe their fiduciary duty to the company as a corporate being in its own right and not to the members individually, not even to a member who is a majority shareholder. Even if a director occupies his position on the board by virtue of another position he holds (for instance, where he is appointed by a major shareholder or is entitled to a seat on the board by virtue of an executive position in the company), a director's fiduciary duties rest upon him as an individual. The fiduciary duty is likewise not owed directly to creditors, employees or other stakeholders of the company, although there is a range of circumstances in which a director may, by virtue of the neglect of his fiduciary duty to the company, be held personally liable to the company's stakeholders.'

In this fiduciary capacity, a director assumes two roles, as an "agent" acting on behalf of the company, and as a trustee who controls company assets.

These roles give rise to the following directors' duties:

— to act in good faith towards the company
— to act only within their powers and use their powers only for purposes which benefit the organization. Directors who act outside their powers bind the company to the transaction but may be held personally liable if a loss results

- not to use for personal gain any information acquired in their capacity as a director
- to act in the best interests of the company and to avoid a conflict between personal and company interests
- to exercise independent judgement in decision-making. A director who is appointed to represent an interest group, for example employees, is nevertheless obliged to act in the best interests of the company as a whole.

Conflict of Interests

A conflict may sometimes arise between a director's personal circumstances and that of the company. The law is unequivocal as to the course of action a director who has a conflict of interests must follow and a director may never prefer his interests over that of the company he is entrusted to direct. A director who does so may be liable to account to the company in respect of any profits he makes as a result of such a transaction.

Directors may often sit on the boards of several companies and conflicts may also arise between the divergent interests of these companies, thus presenting a problem to the individual who sits on the boards of both companies. It is important to note that where a director is simultaneously a director of a holding company and its subsidiary, he owes a separate and distinct fiduciary duty to both entities as legal individuals in their own right. A director must guard against a conflict of interests developing in a situation where he is a director of both the holding company and a subsidiary. Should a conflict arise which prevents him from discharging his duty to both companies properly, he should consider resigning from either or both boards.

Duty of care and skill

The degree of care and skill required is determined objectively by considering how a reasonable person with similar knowledge and experience would have acted, and then comparing this to the director's actions. Each case is considered individually taking into account the nature of the business and the director's specific obligations. As indicated earlier, no distinction is made between executive and non-executive directors.

Statutory Duties

The memorandum of association determines the scope of the company's objects and powers, while the articles of association is a contract between members themselves and between members and the company. The articles therefore contain the internal rules by which a company is governed. The Companies Act provides a standard set of articles that many companies use as a basis but may amend to meet their specific needs. The memorandum and articles are integral to the company and directors should familiarise themselves with their contents since they invariably impose duties on directors.

DIRECTORS AND SHAREHOLDERS

Whilst shareholders retain ultimate responsibility for the company and have the power to remove or not to re-appoint directors, they in effect delegate the day-to-day running of the company to the directors who in turn appoint and supervise management. The board of directors must manage the company within the limits of legislation and the memorandum and articles.

The board may delegate certain powers to managers and at the same time impose appropriate restrictions and conditions which can be varied or revoked at any time. The directors have a duty to monitor management's performance and ensure that management work within their delegated power. In the absence of specific cause for suspicion, directors are generally entitled to trust management to perform their duties honestly and to accept and rely on the judgement, information and advice of management when reaching their own decisions. Directors should not lose sight of the fact, however, that they remain ultimately liable, both jointly as a board and individually, for the well being of the company.

DIRECTORS' POWER TO BIND THE COMPANY

Normally the powers and duties of directors are left undefined and it is implied that directors possess all powers necessary to enable them to direct the affairs of the company. The articles may sometimes seek to limit these powers or to specify particular duties, in which event these limitations must be strictly complied with. A director may not enter into transactions on behalf of the company which are beyond the powers conferred upon him by the articles, the Act and common law.

In some circumstances where directors have acted beyond their powers as directors, the shareholders may subsequently ratify their action by special resolution. Ratification is not possible, however, where the action falls outside the object of the company as defined in the company's memorandum of association. Directors will be liable to the company for any financial losses incurred by it as a result of them having acted outside the scope of their authority.

Any member of the company may institute action against any incumbent or previous director where the company has suffered damages due to a breach of trust or a wrongful act by that director.

LOANS TO DIRECTORS

Loans made either directly or indirectly to directors are prohibited unless:

- all members give their consent
- a special resolution approves a specific loan
- the loan is to enable a director to perform his or her duties
- the business of the company is to make loans
- the loan is to provide assistance to enable the director to participate in a company's share incentive scheme
- the loan is for directors' housing
- the loan is made to a director of a subsidiary who is not also a director of the lending company.

Dissenting Directors

Where a director strongly disagrees with a board decision, he has several ways to indicate this dissatisfaction. A dissenting director may:

- prepare a memorandum setting out his objections
- raise these concerns at a formal board meeting, requesting that a meeting be convened if the matter needs urgent attention and the next board meeting is too late to give proper attention to the issue
- insist on a full hearing at the meeting and request that detailed objections be recorded in the minutes of the meeting
- seek professional advice if this is appropriate.

If the matter is not resolved at a board meeting, the dissenting director could call a general meeting (if authorized by the articles) or rally shareholders to call a general meeting as the shareholders hold the ultimate power in the company. If this is not possible and the director is not prepared to abide by the majority board decision, he may have no alternative but to resign.

RIGHTS OF DIRECTORS

Directors have the right to:

- inspect the company's accounting records, assisted by an accountant
- claim reimbursement for expenses incurred
- discharge their duties without interference from co-directors
- participate in the strategic management of the company and attend and vote at board meetings
- receive reasonable notice of meetings
- take independent professional advice at the expense of the company.

THE BOARD OF DIRECTORS

The minimum number of directors is respectively one for a private, and two for a public company. The maximum number of directors is determined by the company's articles of association. In order not to become unwieldy and ineffective, most boards of public companies are between eight and twelve directors with sixteen being the optimum number recommended for the boards of banks.

The positions of chairperson and chief executive officer of the company should be separated, alternatively that the board appoint a lead independent director who will bring a level of autonomy to board discussions. It also recommends that a board have a majority of non-executive directors. These directors should be totally independent from any significant business relationship with the company since their role is to bring to the board independent judgment and broad business experience.

Role and Function of the Board

The board's role and function is to:

— provide strategic direction to the company
— retain full and effective control of the company
— ensure compliance by the company with all laws and regulations
— communicate with stakeholders in a transparent manner
— delegate appropriate powers to management and monitor the exercise of that delegated power on an ongoing basis
— reserve certain powers to itself as a board where this relates to issues which are material to the company, for instance a change in the strategic focus of the company's business
— have unrestricted access to company information and records
— agree on a procedure to allow directors to obtain independent professional advice where necessary
— review the size and composition of the board in terms of the mix of skills and diversity and decide on the optimal composition required to ensure the board's effectiveness
— identify and monitor key risks and ensure that the company has effective systems of internal control to manage risk within acceptable parameters
— identify key performance areas for the board and management
— identify and monitor non-financial aspects relevant to the company and its stakeholders and ensure that the company conducts itself as a responsible corporate citizen
— record the facts and assumptions which lead it to conclude that the business will be a going concern in the next financial year (and if not, what steps the

board is taking to ensure that this status will be achieved)

- explain the effect of all resolutions required to be passed at shareholders meetings
- ensure the chairpersons of the audit and remuneration committees and as many directors as possible attend shareholders meetings to answer questions about the state of the company
- provide biographies of all directors who are to be appointed at an AGM
- seek the optimum balance for the company between conformance with the dictates of good governance and performance.

Characteristics of an Effective Board

Although directors act in concert as a board, each director is individually responsible for being as effective as he can be. Directors must ensure that they:

- devote adequate time and attention to their duties
- have a good working knowledge of the company, including its organizational structure, management, internal financial controls and its products or services
- prepare adequately for board meetings by working through board and agenda papers
- ensure that management reporting is presented in a clear and easily understood format containing all necessary information about the company that directors need to know
- actively participate in corporate planning including budgeting, strategic planning and cash flow projections

- have access to the entire management team and obtain information from them firsthand where necessary
- assign specific areas of responsibility to management to ensure individual accountability of each manager
- oversee the appointment of senior management and appoint only individuals of suitable calibre
- ensure compliance with relevant legislation and regulations and implement an effective reporting system to monitor such compliance
- conduct visits to company premises on a regular basis
- have a good working knowledge of the contents of important company documents such as the memorandum and articles of association, policy manuals, strategic plans, key contracts, the board charter and the terms of reference of board committees.

Board Charter

Companies consider introducing a charter to govern the performance and operations of the board. A board charter might incorporate details of:

- board composition, proportion of independent directors to other directors, directorship terms and retirement age, and limits on the number of directorships held by each director
- the board's major responsibilities, distinguishing these from management responsibilities
- director selection criteria including skill sets, diversity and experience, recruitment process, and the orientation and induction process to be followed with new directors

— board leadership issues including the selection of the chairman, the separation of roles of the CEO and chairman or the appointment of a lead independent director
— director compenzation
— board meeting procedures
— board performance monitoring and board audits including the assessment of the board and committees' effectiveness and assessment of individual director performance
— guidance on conflicts of interest
— the constitution of Board Committees.

A Charter and Terms of Reference for a company's board and board committees are considered essential for the proper governance of the company.

BOARD AUDITS

Modern companies are highly complex and evolving entities. A director's attention is so often focused on the day-to-day activities of the company that the performance of the board itself may not be questioned until some major event occurs which forces the board to evaluate its effectiveness. The board has a responsibility to ensure that its own performance meets the high standards that it sets for the rest of the company. An analysis of the answers to questions such as those below should be turned into recommendations for incorporation into a strategic plan.

Guidelines on Meeting Procedures

Directors should be prepared to chair a meeting and therefore need to know the basic laws and procedures that apply to meetings. Note that if a technical issue arises, the chairman can always call for an adjournment to seek clarification.

The basics of meeting procedures are:

- give proper and timely notice of a meeting. This means that all those entitled to attend must receive notice within the period prescribed in the Companies Act or the articles of association
- the notice must at least state the time, date and venue, together with the proposed business of the meeting
- before commencing the chairman must ensure that the correct quorum is present and stays present during the meeting. Decisions are invalid if there is no quorum
- notice of the meeting should be read unless a motion is passed that it is to be taken as read
- a motion must have a proposer and usually a seconder too. Not finding a seconder is a strong indication of no other support for the motion
- a good chairman is impartial and allows equal debate on a topic before taking the matter to a vote
- voting usually takes place on a show of hands in which case each person entitled to vote has one vote
- a person entitled to vote may request a ballot (or poll), in which case voting is based on the number of votes each attendee is entitled to cast
- only matters specified on the notice paper may be discussed. New agenda items cannot be added as this prejudices those who are not in attendance
- the chairman usually ends the meeting after the business of the meeting has been concluded.

2

HOW TO BEGIN THE JOB?

HOW TO GET THE JOB?

Traditional job search methods are heavily tended by gatekeepers whose primary function is to keep you from talking to anyone in a position to hire you. Their job is to screen you out. You don't want to put your future in the hands of administrative assistants and clerks. The more diligently you work at your job search, the greater the likelihood you'll wind up with the job you want. Looking for a job is a full-time job in itself. Assuming you're still employed, it means working two jobs at once. Through networking, you find out about opportunities that are not published, budget requisitions in the pipeline for approval, operating needs that will soon be the source of staffing requests, and people who have the authority to hire you on the spot if they think you could help their organization. They don't worry about "approved requisitions" or "money in the budget."

Network Yourself

How can you work the network? Use both e-mail and the telephone, and then follow up, follow up, follow up. Assume that no one will actually do anything they commit to doing without at least three follow-up calls from you. Many people think that networking involves contacting friends and acquaintances for help, or making a list of anyone they've ever known and getting in touch with them. That's true. That's the easy part. Networking also involves cold-calling. Contacting complete strangers. Sometimes, using strangers to refer you to other strangers. The key here is that when you use someone's name, the other person will hardly ever ask you how you know the person whose name you drop. All you'll have to do is say simply, "I was referred to you by . . ." If you *should* be asked how you know the person whose name you dropped, simply say, "I asked them for advice and they suggested. . . ."

A good way to begin the process is to send people an e-mail indicating you'll be calling them within the next few days. It will be very unusual for someone to remember the e-mail, but it gives you a starting point. It also allows you to say to the administrative assistant or other gatekeeper, without completely stretching the truth, that the person you want to reach is "expecting your call." Once you get them on the phone, you want the converzation to go something like this:

— *Introduce yourself with a referral.* "Hello. My name is ________and I'm following up on the e-mail I sent you. Do you recall it? Oh, you don't. I can certainly appreciate the fact that you get many e-mails each day. Well, I was talking with __________and she suggested I contact you."

— *Explain why you're calling.* "I am a_________(recent grad, career changer, industry expert, etc.). I'm looking for some help on _________ (be specific about what you need help on, such as your resume, getting a handle on the job market, learning about the industry, etc.) and __________ (name your referral) tells me that you'd be the perfect person to

_________ (compliment the person you're talking to)."

— *Attempt to appeal to someone you are cold-calling.* Assuming you're talking to a member of top management, check out the company's website. Pick up some information from recent news releases. Go to the employment section. Find that person's biography and read his or her background and accomplishments. Now you're on your way. Talk to the person about:

 — His or her reputation in the industry
 — His or her sense of pride about their company
 — Some accomplishment achieved
 — His or her position in the community
 — The views you share on an important issue
 — A common organization that you belong to (e.g., you graduated from the same alma mater)
 — A shared ethnic background
 — Other shared life experiences.

— *Prove you're worth talking to.* Here's where you have to hook them. For instance, you might say, "I have _________ (give a strong accomplishment that relates to the specific area you want to ask them about). I'm looking for some advice and would really appreciate your help on how to _________ (market myself, write my resume, answer interview questions, prepare a career plan) and wonder if you'd be kind enough to spend maybe fifteen minutes to meet with me."

— *If the person is busy and puts you off, suggest an alternative time.* "I realize how busy you are. Could you spare just a few minutes of your time? I could come in early or meet you late or do it on a weekend. How about ?"

— *If the person says no to meeting, make the most of the phone call.* "Well, I can certainly appreciate the fact that you're too busy to meet. Would you mind if I asked you a couple of quick questions now?"

— *If the person has no time for questions, offer a compromise.* "Well, I can understand how busy you must be. Would you be willing to critique my resume via e-mail? I could send it to you. . . ." (The longer you can keep people on the phone, the more likely they are to agree to meet with you. Give them plenty of opportunity to do that. If they do agree to a meeting, be sure to send them an e-mail confirming the appointment. Many executives rely on someone else to make appointments for them and are very bad about setting appointments on their own.)

— *If they still can't meet with you, ask for a referral.* "Thank you anyhow for taking the time to talk with me. I'm sorry I won't have an opportunity to meet you. I really would have liked that. I can certainly understand why you're not able to give me some help on my resume. Is there anyone else you can think of who may be able to give me some additional advice?"

— *If they can't think of anyone, prompt them with an idea.* "Perhaps an employee of yours or a colleague in another company, or someone from one of the professional associations you belong to. . . ."

— *Close the converzation.* "Thanks for your help. May I call you again sometime, if I'm still looking for advice?" Now you're ready to make your next phone call, and you can start out that converzation by saying, "I was talking to __________ and he suggested I contact you." What if you're actually able to get in to see the person? What then? Well, have a list of questions. Go in with pen and paper in hand. Here are a few ideas about what to ask:

- How did you decide to enter this field?
- What has been your career path? Is that typical for someone in your position?
- What do you like most about your job? What do you like least?
- Do you have any regrets about what you've done in your career?
- What are the important skills that lead to success?
- What am I missing in my background that would help me in this field?
- What professional organizations do you suggest I join?
- What does the trend look like for employment in this field?
- What companies might be interested in someone with my experience? Do you have any contacts there?
- What do you think I should emphasize in my resume? What should I deemphasize?
- What job-search techniques do you recommend?
- What kind of experience do you think I should look for in my next job?
- What conventions or professional meetings should I attend to make more contacts?
- What should I be doing in this field to get more visibility and credibility?
- Is there someone within your organization who might be willing to talk to me?

Always send an e-mail thanking your contacts for their time and telling them how much you appreciate their help. Keep good records on each meeting, too. If one of your contacts says something such as, "Feel free to get back to me if I can be of additional help," then go back to them at a later time, if necessary, and remind them that the two of you spoke.

Attending the Interview

What happens when you get an actual job interview? Be prepared to point out your achievements, show enthusiasm for the organization and the job opportunity, and ask relevant questions that let them know how interested you are.

Interview Don'ts

- Don't complain about anything.
- Don't criticize anyone.
- Don't interrupt.
- Don't give long, confusing answers. A good rule of thumb is that no answer should be longer than a minute. If they want to know more, they'll ask.
- Don't be vague or evasive.
- Don't exaggerate or stretch the truth.
- Don't discuss any personal problems.

Important Interview Do's

- Be early or on time.
- Relax.
- Research the company.
- Be a good listener.
- Talk accomplishments and results.
- Look and act like a professional.

— Prepare questions and answers in advance
— Always be positive. Even with failure experiences, talk about "lessons learned" and how useful the experience was to you in subsequent similar situations.

Here's how to handle the classic interview questions:

— *"Tell me about yourself."* Interviewers don't want to know your life history. They don't care how many brothers or sisters you have or what your hobbies are. This is your chance to give an "elevator pitch." That's a thirty-second summary of what makes you so special. It's as if you were talking to someone on an elevator between floors. Hit them hard and fast with what's special about you and your work experience.
— *"What interests you in this job?"* Here's where you have to make a connection between this opportunity and your career plans. Let them know why it's the next logical step for you. Or give a more general response about how the job will represent a real challenge for you and why you're ready for it.
— *"What interests you in this company?"* Give a prepared response based on the research you've done about the company. Tell them about the growth history and the company's outstanding reputation. Use specifics that you have memorized from the website.
— *"Why should we hire you?"* There are few times where bragging is the right thing to do. This is one of them. Describe your best qualities and give specific examples of the significant things you've been able to do. Say something like, "I know this company is interested in creative, hardworking people. I'd like to think I fit into that category because I've been able to. . . ."

— *"Why are you looking to leave your current company?"* Although you might be tempted to rip apart your manager and the fools who are driving the business into the ground, don't do it. Talk about how you feel it's time to move on, how opportunity is very limited where you work now and you're looking for a new challenge. One of the top reasons people don't get the job is that they come across as complainers. Don't fall into that trap.

— *"What do you like most about your current job?"* In answering this question, make sure that you keep in mind what the job is that you're applying for. Be truthful and talk about the kinds of things you enjoy doing, but always keep it relevant to the job you are applying for.

— *"What are your strengths and weaknesses?"* The first part is a softball question. Succinctly describe the things you do well and be prepared to give examples of accomplishments. You have to be careful on the second part, however. You have to say something. It would be a worst-case scenario if you said, "I have no weaknesses." So, offer up a weakness that isn't really a weakness. For example, you could say, "I sometimes get impatient with people who don't follow through on their commitments." A good interviewer will ask you for a recent example of how you handled that type of situation. Be ready to describe what you did and how there was a successful outcome. The "strengths and weaknesses" question is a cat-and-mouse game. Don't disclose anything that can be used to reject you. If you want to mention a technical weakness, that's fine as long as you talk about what you are doing to get up to speed in that area or it's something that isn't required in the job for which you're applying.

- *"Do you have experience in . . . ?"* If you do, describe clearly and succinctly what your experience has been. Never give a "no" answer to this question. Instead, say something like, "I have done a considerable amount of work in . . . ." Then stress how similar that is to what they're asking about and how easily your skills can be transferred. In short, talk about what you *have* done rather than what you *haven't* done.
- *"What are your salary expectations?"* This is another tricky question that can be used to eliminate you if you're not careful. If there was a stated salary range, you can repeat that back to the interviewer. If not, you can respond with what you're currently earning. A safe response is, "I'm looking to advance my career, and salary would be only one consideration." In general, the less you say on this subject early in the interview process, the better. Once they've decided they want you, *then* you can start to negotiate compenzation.

Interviewing is a lot like selling a product, except, in this case, the product is *you*! Rehearse what you'll say, role-play with others, and video yourself for playback and critique. If you're like most people, you're probably not as well prepared as you should be to present yourself in the best possible light. You want to maximize your chances of getting the job you want.

WHAT TO DO AFTER ACCEPTING THE JOB OFFER

So, you're offered the job you want and you accept it. Congratulations. Now, you're ready to stop celebrating and start performing. Many people are overwhelmed when they get their first management job. They feel their career was on the fast track but now they're trapped in trying to do something they don't know how to do. Some wind up being fired or quitting shortly after being "rewarded" with a promotion into management. There are a lot of reasons people fail, but the biggest reason, in my experience, is that they keep on doing the same things they did before they became a manager.

Moving from individual contributor to manager is a difficult transition to make. It usually involves suddenly going from a senior-level position where you are spending most of your time doing the work to a junior-level management position where you are spending most of your time managing the work. Unfortunately, some people never seem to be able to make the transition. Others were chosen for management because they were outstanding workers. They've been terrific problem-solvers. It's just that they don't know anything about dealing with people. It's like the hardware and software of a computer system. They have to function well together so the computer works flawlessly. So, too, with an organization. The technical work of the department is hard. No question about it. The management work is just as hard. Yet both have to be done.

Many new directors make the mistake of thinking that their people are interested in them. They're not. They're most interested in themselves. When a new director starts, employees have a lot of questions. They want to know how the management change will affect them. They want to know if their job will change. They want to know if this new boss will make their jobs easier or harder.

So, don't come in talking all about yourself. Don't brag about your accomplishments on other jobs. Don't say, "Here's the way we did it back at the XYZ company." It will make people dislike you from the start. It's more important to be an interested person than an interesting person. You'll impress employees the most if you show genuine, sincere interest in them.

For many people, if you're a director, that means you can't be trusted. They're like the cat that Mark Twain describes as jumping on a hot stove. A cat who does that is smart enough to avoid hot stoves for the rest of its life. Unfortunately, it's not smart enough to differentiate between a hot and a cold stove. So, the cat generally avoids all stoves, hot or cold. Some people will say about you, "You'd better not ask questions of the boss. You'll get in trouble." You might ask, "Why would you say that?" Their response might be, "Well, once back in 1983 I got in trouble with a manager, so I've never asked questions since." There are a lot of Twain's cats out there. You've got to earn people's respect and trust. It's not going to be automatically given. They care about your deeds and not your words. As a new manager, it's best to keep the rhetoric to a minimum and look for opportunities to prove yourself.

Recognize *your* new director is on your side. He has a vested interest in your success. Therefore, you're in the best possible bargaining position when you're new to the job. You don't know what can't be done. People are on your side. It's a little like when the country elects a new president. More legislation is typically passed in a president's first year than in the next three years combined. So, go to your director and ask for things. Say, "This is important to my people. I need this." It's unlikely you'll get everything you want. But it's very likely you'll get some of what you want. Remember, you have to *prove* yourself to your people. They want a champion. A warrior. Someone who's willing to battle the bureaucracy. We admire people who have the courage of their convictions. Try to fight the battles you can win. Back off if it's not worth the fight. But now's the time to push back. Your new director wants to please you as much as you want to please her. The honeymoon won't last forever.

When you ask your management for things that are important to your people, avoid weak, tentative language such as, "I think . . ." or "I feel . . ." or "maybe" or "perhaps." That's like asking for a "No!" You increase your chances of getting what you want if you use strong words like "proven," "guarantee," "discover," "results," and "easy." If possible, use surveys, competitive information, and e-mails and other correspondence directly from customers. That way, you're not expressing your personal opinion but you're quoting facts.

Express passion for what you want. Your enthusiasm will be infectious. You can say, "I'd love to prove to you" or "I'd love the opportunity" or "I'd love to have the chance." Make it difficult for your management to say "No!" to you. Often you can tell them that what you're proposing has worked for you in the past or worked elsewhere inside or outside the organization. You can always ask for a "test" or a "trial" to see if it's going to work. Only the most change-averse people will object to that. Be sure to ask for things that are consistent with the company's values and your director's preferences. I can remember having a first converzation with a new director. This person stressed how we have to "get back to basics and do them well." What do you think I did in my second converzation with her? I came in with a "back to basics" proposal. It was as if she said to me, "You had me at hello." Just like a salesperson, use the customer's phraseology, jargon, and way of looking at the world. Ideas don't sell themselves. You've got to sell them.

Companies tend to hire people for a reason. More people are rejected than accepted. If you were chosen for the job, someone must have thought you'd fit in with the values, norms, and culture of the company. The burden is on you, then, to learn the jargon, the way of thinking, and the operating style of the company. Let's clarify these terms:

Values	General ideas about what's good and bad
Norms	Specific expectations about how people should behave
Culture	The pervading system of values and norms

The needs, prejudices, and reward systems in companies and the way they think can be quite different. What one organization prizes, another looks upon with disdain. It's as if you were going to spend some time in a foreign country. What would you do when you first arrive? You certainly would have learned as much as possible even before you got there. You would have researched the country on the Internet and talked to people who have visited or lived there. You'd probably hire a tour guide to show you around when you first arrived. You'd learn the local ways of doing things so you wouldn't stand out in a crowd as an "outsider."

For example, imagine if you were a woman staying at the Intercontinental Hotel in the strict Islamic city of Dacca, the capital of Bangladesh. There is a sign inside the hotel that says, "Ladies in shorts may be stoned." No, that doesn't refer to drug use. It means that people would be within their legal rights to throw rocks at a woman wearing shorts until they killed her. If you drove a rental car too fast in Singapore, you could be subject to a $5,000 fine for speeding. A popular T-shirt that young people wear in Singapore says, "Singapore is a fine country." Now you understand the way they mean it. The last thing you'd ever do if you went into a foreign country is try to change their culture overnight.

The old-fashioned view of an organization was as a pyramid where the people at the top are the important ones. Information would flow one way—downward. The planning, organizing, controlling, and directing were all done at the top. The job of a subordinate was simply to support the wishes of management. Often, people would get a sore neck because they looked one way virtually all the time—upward. Employees existed to serve their director. A more modern view of an organization is as an upside-down pyramid, as shown in Figure 1.

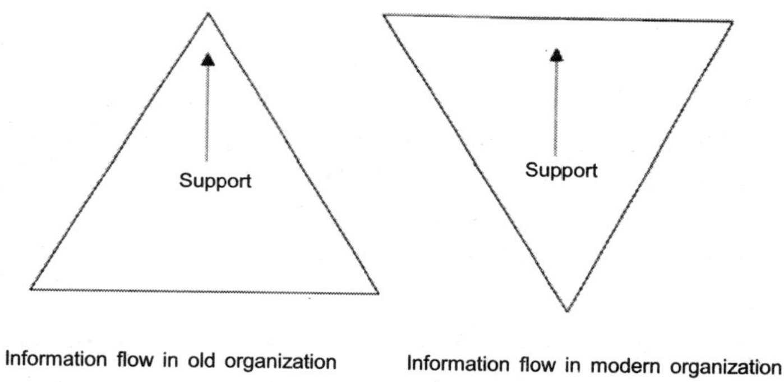

Figure 1. Information flow in the old vs. modern organization.

The people at the top (the employees) are the important ones. They make the product, sell the product, service the product, and work with customers on a day-to-day basis. Information should flow two ways—upward and downward. The job of the director is to support the employees. Directors should get a sore neck because they should look one way most of the time—downward. They exist to ensure the success of their employees.

You can show employees that they're critically important to you on your first day of work by having a group meeting. Don't make the mistake of thinking your role should be to tell the people all about your expectations of them. Just the opposite. It would be better to find out what their expectations are of you. Be humble and gracious. First impressions are important. You want to get off to a good start. Therefore, you should focus on them and not on yourself. The more you know about the department, the better off you'll be. Tell your employees how pleased you are to be part of this group. Tell them you've heard good things about them. If you're able to list some of their major accomplishments, they'll think you're wonderful. Remember, it's about them (the employees) and not about you (the director). Why don't directors understand this simple concept?

Job Stages

All directors will pass through a series of stages when they begin a new job. The pattern is always the same. Sometimes a stage takes a long time to get through. Other times, a director can get stuck on a stage and never progress. But every director passes through these four stages:

1. *Investigation.* The more research you do before actually accepting a job, the better off you'll be. This investigative work includes finding out exactly what the job is and isn't. It also includes determining what has been accomplished or not accomplished up to now and why. It should involve understanding the political climate and learning about the people you'll be working for and working with.
2. *Initiation.* This is the period of confusion when you're trying different approaches to getting things done. It's when you test people to find out what the underlying issues and political sensitivities are. It's also a time when people test you out to see what you're made of. They'll say things like, "The old director let me. . . ." In truth, it never really happened. They want to see what they can get away with. Initiation can be an uncomfortable period when it appears there's no way you can learn what you need to know. Invariably, you'll

step in some bear traps because you didn't know important background information.

3. *Acceptance.* Now you've adjusted. You've learned about your environment. You understand the informal organization and people regard you as a full-fledged participant. You're familiar with the department and company jargon and what you can realistically hope to accomplish.
4. *Contribution.* Only after you've gone through the first three stages can you really be of significant benefit to the organization. This is the stage when you begin to produce results and really earn your money. How quickly you get to this stage as a director depends on how hard you've worked and how astute you've been in navigating through the first three stages.

FIRST MEETINGS WITH EMPLOYEES

The biggest thing for you to do from your first moments on the job is to project confidence and optimism. If you're not confident, you must still *act* confident. If it's a problem department with a poor track record, then don't tell them you've heard good things about them and list their accomplishments. Instead, talk about how you're looking forward to the challenge that the job holds in store. Whatever the case, tell people how much you'll be relying on them. Establish the fact that you'll need their cooperation and commitment for success. It would be good if your boss attended at least the first part of the meeting to introduce you and talk about your background. If anyone is going to do any bragging about you, it should be your new boss. If people start to bring up problems, tell them that's exactly the kind of information you'll be looking for in your one-on-one meetings with them. Do not let this first meeting degenerate into a gripe session.

It'll be important for you to identify the opinion leaders of the group. They may have formal titles, but often they are just senior people that the others look up to. Be very deferential and respectful. Tell them how important they are to you and, if you can, run things past them before you present them to the group at large. These people will love it if you ask for their help and advice. When you say something, the more junior people will turn to these leaders and say, "What do you think?" You'd better have them on your side. You want them to say one thing and one thing only: "This new director is good. I'm impressed."

You've got to take the time to build relationships up, down, and across the organization. Recognize that what matters is who you've been able to create alliances with. Grade levels, job descriptions, and organization charts are of little importance. If someone wants to ignore you, they will. If someone wants to put you at the top of their priority list, they'll do that, too.

During one of my seminars, a new director once told me about his first assignment: He was going to Ireland to force those people to adhere to certain corporate manufacturing standards. His boss told him to go out there and establish his authority. I told him that he was going on a suicide mission. He didn't understand why. I said, "By all means, go to Ireland, but you've got to earn credibility. People have to see you as an ally and not as a threat." I told him to spend time at the pub with the employees. "They'll tell you about the problems they're having with corporate," I said. "They'll tell you about how no one got back to them on this and how they don't know the status of that. There will be some easy things you can do for them. First, earn their respect. Then you can ask them for help."

Schedule one-on-one meetings to begin to establish a relationship with each person working for you. Ask them if they'd like to continue these meetings on a monthly or quarterly basis. Ask the same general questions of everyone:

- How is the job going?
- What are the things you like and don't like about the job?
- What are your expectations of me?
- What's the best way for me to get to know what you do?
- Do you have any career plans or individual development plans that I should know about?
- Is there anything in particular that I can do for you?

Stress the same things you did in the group meeting. Express confidence and tell your employees how much you need their help and support. It would be great if you've done your homework and can personalize your comments; then you can say something like, "Jim, I understand you're the person who was responsible for the product innovation that led to . . . ." A lot of this homework should be done before you even start the job. If you can memorize people's names, job responsibilities, and accomplishments, it will help you get off to a really good start. Contrast this with the director who comes in totally unprepared, gets people's names wrong, doesn't understand who does what, and knows nothing of the group's history. What a difference!

Be sure to take notes so that you'll remember who said what. It'll be very impressive days or weeks from now if you say to someone, "As you mentioned in our first one-on-one meeting . . . ." Don't feel you have to explain or defend anything that has happened in the past. If someone brings up past transgressions by the previous director, simply listen attentively.

Be sure to use the person you are replacing as a resource, too. Even if previous directors left the company, seek them out after you've had the first group meeting and the first set of one-on-ones with employees. Anyone who previously held your position can help you interpret what people are saying and why. They'll also tell you about the mistakes they made with the group and what they found to be the best way to work with each of the people. You can also use new bosses this way. Ask them to interpret the things the people are telling you.

Make sure you and your new boss discuss goals and expectations. You may have to push back when your director starts to pile projects on you. It's possible that you'll have to say, "I need to meet with the staff as well as internal customers. I need to understand the work and how it gets done. Is there a way we could prioritize these projects?" Make sure you meet frequently with your new director to learn her views on your department mission, goals, and expectations. Establish strong lines of communication with your director from the beginning.

Hopefully, you've already done research to find out what your new boss's preferences and prejudices are. After all, the boss carefully checked your references. Shouldn't you have checked the boss's as well? You should talk to current and former subordinates of that director. You should talk to reputable employment agencies and those in professional associations. You should find out his track record on developing people, encouraging innovation, and granting autonomy, for example. Don't let the director give you textbook answers about philosophy. Ask for specifics on what the director has done in the past. The company has made a big investment in you. You're making an even bigger investment in them.

Seek out the unsuccessful candidates for your job, especially if they'll be working for you, because they can affect your future performance. Put yourself in their shoes. Acknowledge their feelings. Then, take the offensive. If appropriate, tell them you'll make every effort to use their expertise and experience. Acknowledge that you need their commitment in order to succeed. If you're really good, you'll be aware of their achievements and can quote them. Ask them if there's anything in particular you can do for them. Obviously, if they are working directly for you, you are in a position to give them the experience and training they may need to enhance their candidacy for your position or a position like it. If you know they are highly regarded by others in management, by all means tell them that. The worst thing you can do is tell them how good *you* are. The best thing you can do is tell them how good *they* are. As a new person, you need all the friends you can get. You don't need enemies lurking around waiting to pounce on you.

If someone expresses resentment that you were hired or promoted or about having to "train" you, always indicate that you understand the way the person feels. Don't ever try to defend why you were chosen for the job. That wasn't your decision to make. Try and pivot the discussion from what has already happened to what can happen in the future. Indicate confidence in them, stressing how important they will be to you and how much you will need their help. If there is anything in particular you can do for the person (e.g., getting them involved in a certain project or with new technology), tell them you'll try to do that. Don't make promises you can't keep. That will hurt your relationship with them in the long run. Also, never argue with a resentful person. Never tell them they shouldn't feel the way they feel. They're already angry. You'll never win the argument. Instead, listen attentively and empathize with them. Try to be on their side, as much as possible.

Always use the "clean slate" approach with people. If they were known to have performance problems, tell them it doesn't matter to you what's happened in the past. You can turn around many supposed bad attitudes this way. If they had a bad relationship with the old director, just tell them you don't know anything about that and you're starting fresh with them.

You've got one very important factor working in your favour as a new director. You are your boss's choice. Your boss wants you to succeed. You also don't know the constraints on you because you just got there. Therefore, you're in an ideal position to ask for things. You're also likely to *get* them. So, be assertive. It will be difficult for your boss to say "No!" to you. Go in and say, "My people are very concerned about . . ." or "My people are pretty angry that . . ." or "My people say they really need. . . ." Look for the low-hanging fruit. The easy things that will prove to people that you've listened to them and you're responding. You won't be able to get *everything* you want. On the other hand, it's likely that you'll get *some* of what you want.

WAY OF EFFECTIVE COMMUNICATION

Establish a culture of open, two-way communication. The less information given to employees, the more active the company grapevine. Rumours, gossip, half-truths, innuendo, exaggeration, and facts get mixed together to fill a communication vacuum. While management is in meetings trying to figure out what to say to the troops, the troops usually know the story already and are trying to guess what kind of tale management will tell.

Be sure to look for small wins for your group. At the beginning, try to have your group take on easy projects that give them a sense of accomplishment. Save the big stuff for later. Do everything you can to make people feel like winners. Make sure their accomplishments are recognized. Early success will breed more success for you and your group.

Continue to hold regular group meetings. Recognize, however, that if there's a universal complaint, it's that there are too many meetings, they're too long, and they accomplish too little. In some companies, it seems that individual responsibility is avoided by calling meetings to talk about problems. The problems don't get solved. It's just that people can say, "Oh, yes. We had a meeting about that."

So, it's not just about running meetings. It's about running worthwhile, carefully planned meetings. It starts with coming up with the answers to these questions:

— *Objective.* What key results do you want the meeting to achieve? Don't just have a staff meeting to have a staff meeting. There should be a purpose to the meeting. If a meeting isn't necessary, then don't have it.

— *Timing.* How long should the meeting last? When is the best time to conduct it?

— *Participants.* Who should attend? Include people with decision-making authority, people whose commitment is wanted, and people who have a need to know.

— *Agenda.* What items should be dealt with? How will participants help in preparing the agenda? Who will distribute it? It really helps if the agenda is an ambitious one. Putting too many items into too little time will help people focus. The meeting leader can also say, "We've got a lot to cover. Let's try to stay on track."

— *Ground Rules.* What are the rules of conduct for the meeting? Think of the things that typically go wrong in your meetings and come up with agreed-upon ground rules. You may want to post those ground rules in the meeting room.

– *Physical Arrangements.* What facilities and equipment are required? How should the room be set up? Should we use Net Meeting, Live Meeting, or some other form of technology?
– *Role Assignments.* Who'll be the note-taker, timekeeper, discussion moderator, etc.?
– *Evaluation Method.* How will the meeting be evaluated in order to improve it for next time?

HOW TO BE AN EFFECTIVE DIRECTOR?

Know Your Role

Being an effective director begins with knowing (1) the role of the board for the business you are serving, and (2) the specific reason you were asked to serve. For private companies, the role of the board is frequently more advisory than governance, so it is a good idea to ask the owners or others inviting you to join them to clarify exactly what they expect from the board. There are various types of boards, ranging from "window dressing" to more active boards that actually govern through strategic and/or specific operational duties.

In nearly every board, the time perspective of relevance is more long-term than short-term. That is, boards should typically take the view of where is the company heading in the long-term, and what strategies do we have to get there? This long-term attitude is what owners of private companies usually need to hear—they are usually doing all they can to keep up with the current day-to-day struggles of running the business. In private companies, boards really serve at the pleasure of the owner/entrepreneur, so be sensitive and listen to what is asked of you, and try to respond to those specific requests—and leave the backseat driving to others—at least until you have earned the respect needed to offer constructive observations and criticisms.

Directors also need to know their personal role within the board forum. Rarely is a prima donna director effective. Boards function best when the members work together as a team. Some directors falsely assume that since they are now directors, they must be experts in everything. Not true! A good director will realize that his or her opinion is very useful for some matters, somewhat useful for other issues, and *not useful at all* for some issues. The important thing is for the board as a whole to realize its role, and then for individual directors to participate according to their abilities to serve the group.

Allow for an Orientation Period

Whether joining a new or established board, some orientation period will be necessary before a new member will feel comfortable, at home, and accepted. Some new directors may even experience a period of ritualistic "hazing" by some of the old-timers. These rituals, however, are usually quite harmless, and may even contribute positively to building friendships, trust, respect, and esprit-de-corps. The orientation period will go a little more smoothly if the new director takes it all in stride and with good humour. In fact, the new director will earn respect more quickly by showing a little humility towards others who probably have more experience and certainly more seniority. The new director also needs to avoid coming into a board with a loaded agenda and an attitude that says "I'm here to save you and correct all the mistakes you have made." Certainly, few directors would say this verbally, but the attitude is sometimes conveyed. Sure, the new director was recruited to bring some new ideas and perspective to the board, but one should never come into a new situation and try to make changes the first day, or even the first few meetings.

Be Professional

A professional attitude and work style will go a long ways toward building an effective tam. Professionalism means many things. It means being prepared for board meetings, including reviewing carefully your agenda and meeting packet before the meeting begins. A directly quickly skimming over an agenda and financial statements while the chairman is calling the meeting to order is giving him or herself away as unprepared. This is rude, and other directors who are prepared will not appreciate it—especially if it is a pattern, and not a one-time event.

Professionalism also means being on time for the meeting and being prepared to stay until the meeting is adjourned! Directors who always have to leave early are often labeled as less committed – so their professional perception suffers. Believe it or not, professionalism even means getting enough sleep the night before so as to be alert and not yawning during someone's comments or presentation. Another point about professionalism is good to remember—the importance of having good manners. In this day and time, it seems as though some people have forgotten the simple virtue of politeness. The use of simple courtesies, such as "please, thank you, you're welcome, and I am sorry," go a long way toward building trust and respect. Likewise, cursing, vulgar jokes, personal attacks, wasting time with irrelevant chatter, and negative behaviors of all types will destroy whatever harmony may have existed in a group. Be polite, and you are well on your way to being a professional director.

Participate

A director may be the most brilliant and successful member of the community, but if he or she does not participate, that talent is of little use to a board of directors. Good boardroom participants are prepared, they listen to others, and they share their views, opinions, and experiences. They are sensitive to the opinions of others, yet they avoid "groupthink," or going along with the crowd just to avoid controversy. Directors should periodically assess their participation in meetings. A little honest self-reflection can do wonders to keep individual participation levels at an appropriate level—and in balance with the other board members.

Seek Feedback

Unfortunately, board memberships do not typically have a formal job description or annual performance appraisal. In fact, the structure of the board for many private companies is so informal that an appointment is often assumed to be a "life term" with no questions asked.

Absent from any formal review process, each director should seek outside feedback to ensure that their performance is satisfactory, and, hopefully, ever-improving. A good place to start is to simply ask the chairman, or CEO to honestly tell you what they think about your effectiveness as a director. Try to avoid catching them off-guard or on-the spot—perhaps suggest a lunch or breakfast meeting and let them know in advance what you want to talk about.

Another good source of feedback can come from fellow directors. Your peers will view you differently than the company leadership. Simply tell another director that you are doing a self-evaluation and want some feedback on how they think you are performing as a directly. You will probably be pleasantly surprised how positively this sort of question is received.

If you are not Contributing, Resign!

Getting asked to serve on a board is a great experience. You feel positive about yourself, as someone else expresses confidence in your ability to contribute at such a high level of responsibility. Sometimes, however, the director-elect can confuse flattery with "fit". Just because you have an invitation does not necessarily mean it is right for you. Many boards have at least one board member who really should not serve—not necessarily because the director is incompetent, but because it is just not a good fit for the person or the company. Don't let that board member be you!

Be Effective

One last thought about effectiveness: do not accept an invitation to serve unless you really think you can contribute—and you intend to work hard to do so. And, after some interval of board service you feel you are not contributing, resign and get out of the way—you will be less frustrated finding a better place to serve and the board will be healthier, too.

❖❖❖

3

REFORMS IN DIRECTORS' JOB

A very important part of 'core company law' is the rights and duties of key corporate participants i.e., those who manage or direct the affairs or business of the company on behalf of investors/ shareholders; these directors who have the necessary skill and expertise to steer the company towards long-term sustainability. In Malaysia, as with other common law jurisdictions, the responsibility for managing the affairs the company is placed with the company's board of directors, who have a collective responsibility.

Notwithstanding the existence of market forces which operate to discipline directors, there is still a need for legal controls over directors' conduct. A study of various jurisdictions indicates that there are several approaches or strategies that can be adopted by the law to promote 'accountability' of those who manage the affairs of the company. These approaches, amongst other things, include having in place an effective disclosure regime, ensuring that shareholders can remove errant directors before the completion of their tenure in office, regulating transactions entered into by the company with directors and persons related/connected to the directors, enhancing the shareholders rights to remedy corporate abuses and of course clarifying and reformulating directors duties. It is to be noted that these approaches do not apply in isolation and in most cases are complementary of each other.

One important legal mechanism for ensuring directors' accountability is the imposition of duties on directors. Reform exercises in comparable jurisdictions indicate that there is a similarity of objectives in reforming directors' duties and that is to ensure an appropriate balance between legal rules that ensure directors' accountability and legal rules that may stifle appropriate risk-taking by directors.

Shareholders' interests have always been the paramount consideration as far as directors' duties are concerned. However, there is an increasing call for reform in this area of the law where reform exercises in other comparable jurisdictions have resulted in company law legislations that have incorporated provisions which expressly require directors to consider the interest of other stakeholders.

Incorporation of such provisions requires a change in mindset for, traditionally, company law has only been only concerned with the interest of the company's shareholders and to a certain extent with the interest of the company's creditors.

Reform exercises in comparable jurisdictions indicate that there are two approaches to specifying the board's role and functions.

One approach is to incorporate a provision to that effect in the company legislation. Australia and New Zealand have adopted this approach. Their respective company legislations set out a general statement of the board's role and function and that statement provides that the role and function of the board is to manage or supervise the affairs of the company.

The alternative approach is to set out the role and functions of the board outside the company legislation, for example, by way of a provision in the Articles of Association or by way of the codes of best practises as is practised in the UK.

Clarification of directors' duty of care, skill and diligence and directors fiduciary duties Clarification of the law on directors' duties is very much needed to enable the law to keep abreast of changes in the commercial and business environment. In many instances the duties imposed by the law on directors is influenced by standards of conduct that the public expects of directors. Publicity of recent corporate scandals have raised concerns that the legal rules may not be clear or strict enough to prevent or minimize potential breaches of duties imposed on directors. However, it must also be pointed out in the above mentioned corporate scandals, glaring conflicts of interest situation and mismanagement did not go unpunished.

Legal standards of behaviour must keep abreast with the public's expectation and specifically in respect to standards regulating corporate behaviour. Those standards must also conform to established business practises otherwise the legal standards will not facilitate business.

It is not an easy task to make the legal standards of behaviour conform with established business practises as some business practises may not be so clear cut and can also at times be in conflict with the legal standard of conduct that are imposed on directors. For example, it is a common business practise to appoint nominee directors to represent specific interests on the company's board or for a person to be a director in several companies belonging to the same corporate group. However, strict duty requires a director to act only in the interest of the company of which he is a director.

DELEGATION AND SUPERVISION

It is a known fact that in larger companies, directors do not actually manage the company but in fact merely carry out a supervisory role. The actual management function is left to others (the managers of the company) and it is these persons who the directors are said to supervise.

Hence, delegating management function to others and relying on others has become the norm in the way directors manage the affairs of the company, especially in respect to large companies.

The question, however, is whether the delegation of functions to others and reliance on others by directors should provide directors with a shield from being made accountable for mismanagement or wrongs committed by the delegate or, in other words, should directors be allowed to pass the buck to the delegate.

Cross jurisdictional studies on corporate law reform in other jurisdictions indicate that there is a trend in making sure that although directors may have the right to delegate and rely on others, directors ultimately should remain accountable for the actions of their delegates, except where the director has exercised due diligence over the delegate.

PROTECTION OF HONEST DIRECTORS

Promoting the accountability of those who manage the affairs of the company not only means that there must be an imposition of liabilities for breaches of duty but there must also be protection afforded to the honest director.

Cross jurisdictional studies on corporate law reform in other jurisdictions indicate that a common approach used by corporate law in other jurisdictions to encourage proper persons to take up directorship is to extend immunity to those directors who have acted honestly and exercised appropriate standards of due diligence whilst carrying out their stewardship function.

In some countries, this approach has resulted in the enactment of a business judgment rule which provides a safe harbour to such directors.

The above are some of the important issues that permeate the discussion on directors' duties. The task of clarifying and reformulating directors' duties so as to promote accountability is not an easy one but it has to be done so as to ensure that our corporate law framework remains effective and can facilitate businesses.

DIRECTORS' RESOLUTION

A resolution is the record of a decision or intention that is made during a meeting. There are two types of resolutions—directors' resolutions and members' resolutions. Members' resolutions can be further separated into ordinary or special resolutions. All resolutions passed in the course of a meeting must be entered into the minutes book and may also have to be lodged with the company, depending on the type of resolution and its purpose.

Also known as Board Resolutions, these resolutions are usually passed by a simple majority of votes at a Board Meeting. In the case of a deadlock, the Chairman of the meeting is often given a casting or second vote to resolve the matter if provided in the Articles.

Examples of directors' resolutions include:

- Opening of bank account
- Appointment of company officers
- All other resolutions which need not be passed by a Special Resolution as indicated in the Companies Act or the company's Articles

Directors' Resolution by Circulation

To make it easier to pass resolutions for routine decisions, your company's Articles of Association ("Articles") may contain an article to allow for directors' resolutions to be passed by written means. This means the resolution can be prepared on paper and circulated to all of your co-directors so that they can vote with their signatures. If the required majority of directors sign in approval of the resolution, it will be deemed valid and will have equal status as any that is passed at a Board Meeting. If your company has directors situated in different locations, the same article may allow for copies of the resolution to be circulated to them too. Appendices, correspondences and documents to the resolution should be kept as attachments in the minutes book.

Members' Resolutions

Decisions of members are made by passing resolutions. Members are allowed to exercise their decision-making power by voting on ordinary resolutions and special resolutions. The matters on which members are allowed to vote for can be found in your company's Memorandum or Articles.

Ordinary Resolution

An ordinary resolution is a resolution that has been passed by a simple majority of over 50% of the votes cast by members entitled to vote, either in person or by proxy at the meeting.

Special Resolution

A special resolution is a resolution that fulfills the following conditions:

1. Has been passed by not less than 75% of the votes cast by members entitled to vote, either in person or by proxy at the meeting; and
2. A written notice of the special resolution has been given to members of your company. If your company is a private company, members must be given at least 14 days written notice. If it is a public company, at least 21 days' written notice is required; and
3. The notice must announce the intention to propose that the resolution involved be tabled as a special resolution.

Some instances where a special resolution is required are as follows:

— Alteration of Object Clauses in Memorandum

— Alteration of Articles

— Change in company name

— Reduction of share capital

— Voluntary winding up

— Removal of liquidator in a voluntary winding up

Members' Resolution by Written Means

Similar to a directors' resolution, members' resolutions may also be passed by written means if your company's Memorandum and Articles does not prohibit it. A private company with few shareholders may find this provision useful as it saves the company from having to hold a general meeting when decisions have to be made. The resolutions can be circulated in paper form or other form agreed upon between the company and the shareholders e.g. e-mails. A member(s) holding 5% of votes can, within 7 days after the resolution is circulated, request a general meeting instead. The requisite number of members entitled to attend and vote at a general meeting would have to sign or agree with the resolution for it to be considered as effectively passed. For one-member companies, the sole member may simply record and sign the resolution by himself. All members are to be notified that the resolution has been passed within 15 days.

Lodgement of Resolutions

The Companies Act requires that certain types of resolutions be lodged. Unless otherwise stated in the Act, every special resolution passed or every resolution which binds any class of shareholders must be lodged within one month after its passing. Other than that, an ordinary resolution to allot shares is also required to be lodged.

CAPITAL MAINTENANCE

The law provides that a company cannot use its share capital except for the purposes of trading and conducting business. As such, one of the things it cannot do is to return any of its assets to the members except in the form of dividends which are to be paid out of profits. It is only under a few circumstances that a company is allowed to alter or reduce its share capital in the situations explained in the following sections.

Share Capital Alteration

A company may alter its share capital if allowed by its Articles. The following are some of the alterations that can be made:

- Consolidating and dividing share capital;
- Converting paid-up shares into stock and reconverting the same stock back into paid-up shares;
- Subdividing shares. The proportion between the amount paid and amount unpaid on each reduced share must remain the same;

- Cancel shares which at the date of resolution have not been taken or agreed to be taken; or
- Cancel unissued capital or shares which have been forfeited.

Reduction of Share Capital by a Private Company

A company can reduce its share capital only if the company's Articles do not expressly prohibit it to do so. Share capital can be reduced in the following ways:

- Cancel or reduce liability on shares that has not been paid up;
- Cancel share capital that has been paid up but is no longer represented by available assets; or
- Return to members paid-up share capital that is no longer required by the company.

There are two ways in which reduction of a company's capital is permitted—one with court sanction and the other without. Both these methods require a special resolution to be passed before they can be initiated. A copy of the resolution must then be lodged with the Registrar.

Under the frst method, the company's special resolution to reduce capital is submitted for approval by the Court. If the company intends to reduce capital without seeking approval from the Court, it can do so but must meet the solvency and publicity requirements as prescribed.

It is advisable for you to seek professional advice if your company intends to reduce its share capital.

Transfer of Shares

Shares are personal property, and every shareholder enjoys the right to transfer his shares to anyone, although subject to the limitations as imposed by the particular company's Articles of Association.

Restrictions on Share Transfers

The two most common forms of restrictions to share transfer are:

(a) The need for approval by the Board of Directors, which is granted by the passing of a board resolution at a board meeting; or

(b) The presence of a pre-emption clause in the Articles specifying that any member who intends to sell his shares must first offer them to other current members. The procedure to be followed for this will be as prescribed in the Articles.

Refusal to Register Transfer

The Article can provide that it is the right of directors to refuse the transfer of shares that have not been fully paid up, to a person whom they do not approve, or for shares on which the company has a legal right to claim for any reason. A company can also refuse to register a share transfer. In such a case, notice of refusal must be given to the seller ("transferor") and the recipient ("transferee") within one month after the date the transfer documents are lodged with the company.

Share Transfer Procedures

Do note that transfer of shares by way of gift, by sale or for reason of asset distribution are liable for stamp duty in India. The Stamp Duty rate is 0.2% of the Consideration or Net Asset Value, whichever results in a higher amount.

Generally, the proper procedure to be adopted for the transfer of shares is as follows:

(a) Check the Articles for rules on share transfers and ensure that pre-emption rights (if any) have either been fulfilled or waived.

(*b*) Ensure that the transfer documents are signed by both the transferor and transferee.

(*c*) Present the transfer documents and relevant share certificates to the company.

(*d*) Pass a board resolution approving the share transfer.

(*e*) Present the documents for stamping and pay the stamp duty.

(*f*) Update Registers of Members.

(*g*) Cancel old share certificates and issue new ones.

h. File a "Notice by Local Company of Transfer of Shares/ Change in Particulars of Shareholders" with ACRA.

Share Certificates

A certificate bearing the common seal of the company is proof of a member's ownership of the shares. Every share certificate should state under seal all of the following details:

(*a*) Date of issue

(*b*) Name of the company

(*C*) The authority under which the company is constituted, i.e. Singapore

(*d*) Address of the company's Registered Office

(*e*) Class of shares

(*f*) Name of the registered member

(*h*) Number of shares

(*i*) Certificate number.

If you are named as a member in the company's register, you will be entitled to receive share certificates free of charge. However, if the shares are held jointly by several persons, the company need only issue one certificate to be delivered to one of the shareholders. Every company should ensure that all necessary share certificates are issued and delivered promptly. The timeline is within two months after a share has been issued, or within one month after a completed share transfer is lodged with the company.

FIDUCIARY DUTIES OF A DIRECTOR

To carry out your duties as a director well, it is necessary for you to be fully aware of the duties and responsibilities expected of directors.

Directors are fiduciaries of the company which appoints them. A fiduciary is a person who is expected to act in the interests of another person. Hence, as a director, you have a duty to act in the way you honestly believe to be in the best interest and benefit of the company.

Directors are also agents of the company. This means that you are acting for the company and in turn, the company is bound by your acts. Thus, it is important for you to exercise reasonable skill, care and diligence when carrying out your duties as a director.

The duties owed by directors to a company are found in the common law and the Companies Act. The following are some key duties which will be discussed in greater detail:

- To act honestly and in good faith in the interest of the company
- To avoid conflict of interest
- To exercise care, skill and diligence
- To not misuse power and information
- Differences between Common Law and Statutory Law duties

There is a considerable overlap between the common law duties and statutory duties. The differences between the two are defined as follows:

Common Law duties	*Statutory Law duties*
Found in cases.	Found in the Statutes.
Enforced by the company.	Enforced by regulators or taken up by persons aggrieved by your actions.
Breach will result in civil liabilities and remedies.	Breach may result in criminal prosecution and/or civil action, and criminal and civil sanctions
The company can ratify breaches of common law duties. The court can also excuse breaches.	The company cannot stop the regulator from prosecuting the director if there is a breach.

If you are unsure if you will breach your duty as a director to the company when making disclosures, you should seek further professional advice on the matter.

Duty to Act Honestly

One of a director's key fiduciary duties is to act honestly and in good faith for the best interest of the company. It is important for you and your co-directors to give undivided loyalty to the company. Decisions should be made in the interest of the company and any personal or third party's interests should be disregarded. Directors will be held liable if they have acted without first considering the interests of the company.

As a director, it is important for you to act honestly at all times when carrying out your duties. When dealing with your co-directors, you should be honest by telling the whole truth and not to hide any material facts. You should also declare any personal conflict of interest to the board voluntarily so as to ensure transparency. Any attempt to defraud the company or gain an advantage for oneself or others at the expense of the company will amount to dishonesty, and may result in civil action or criminal prosecution or both.

Certain transactions undertaken by directors which are not profitable can still be in the interest of the company. Examples include sponsorships or charitable donations. Even though these transactions do not generate profit, they may be commercially benefcial because they serve to enhance the company's corporate image.

Facts which lead to a breach under the common law may also amount to a breach under statutory law. This may in turn result in both civil and criminal liabilities. Hence, it is beneficial for you as a director to at all time act honestly and in good faith for the best interest of the company.

Duty to Avoid Conflicts of Interest

Under both common and statutory law, a director should not place himself in a position where the interests of the company come into conflict with his personal interest. It is therefore important for you as a director to be familiar with the common circumstances where conflicting interests may arise. It is also necessary for you to be aware of disclosure requirements applicable if you should find yourself in any of these circumstances.

The following are some instances where there may be conflicting interests:

1. Transactions with company

An instance where conflicting interests may arise is when the director directly or indirectly enters into transactions with the company, for example, buys from or sells property to the company.

2. Taking advantage of corporate information and opportunities

Directors are not allowed to take over corporate property such as business opportunities and information without the permission of the company. For instance, directors are not allowed to divert business intended for the company to themselves or a third party. A director who sets up another firm to rival and compete for contracts with the company will also have breached his fiduciary duties.

Even if the company lacks the necessary expertise or resources to take advantage of an opportunity (e.g. lack of financial resources), there is no excuse for a director to divert that opportunity elsewhere because it still belongs to the company.

Also, even if a director resigns, he does not have the right to take advantage of any business opportunity that have been made available to the company. This will still result in a breach of his duty as he obtained knowledge of the opportunity while serving as a director in the company.

3. Conficting duties

Directors may sometimes have conflicting duties as they may be serving as directors of more than one company. There may be potential conflict of interest arising from the various directorships held by the director. Hence, it is important for the director to make disclosure to all the companies concerned informing them of his various directorships. The declaration must be made to the company's board at the first meeting the director attends after he is appointed. Such a disclosure must be recorded in the minutes of the meeting.

In practice, it is common for directors of competing companies to absent themselves from board room meetings and discussions of matters in which they may face a confict of interest or duties.

4. Nominee director

A nominee director is a person appointed to represent

the interests of another group or person. For instance, a nominee director may be appointed to sit in a board by a substantial shareholder or a special class of shareholders.

Nominee directors may often find themselves in a dilemma as to whose interest to represent. The Act allows a nominee director to divulge information to his appointer only if he fulfils the following conditions:

(a) He must declare at a meeting of directors, the name and office or position held by the person whom the information is to be disclosed to.

(b) He must also declare the particulars of the information which he intends to disclose.

(c) He must receive authorization from the board before making such a disclosure.

(d) He must ensure that the disclosure will not in any way prejudice the company.

Disclosure requirement

If a director should find himself in a position of conflict, he is required to make full and proper disclosure to the company regarding this. If no such disclosure is made, the director will have breached his duty to avoid a conflict of interest.

Under the common law, the director must disclose his conflicting interests to the company at the general meeting. Under the statutory law, the disclosure must be made at a meeting with the board.

In practice, in their Articles some companies provide that the disclosure requirement as prescribed in the common law will be deemed to have been complied with when disclosure has been made to the board of directors.

Disclosure of transactions with the company

If a director is interested in any of the transactions the

company is undertaking or considering, he must make the appropriate disclosure to the board. The disclosure should be made at a directors' meeting and must be recorded in the minutes.

Disclosure of conflict arising from holding other offices

A director must make disclosure if he holds any office or property where his interests are in conflict with his duties as a director in the company. At a meeting of the directors, he has to declare the fact, nature, character and extent of the conflict and this disclosure must be recorded in the minutes.

Duty of Care, Skill and Diligence

Under both the common law and statutory law, directors are expected to exercise reasonable care, skill and diligence in managing the company. Section 157 of the Act specifically emphasises that Directors are required to act honestly and use reasonable diligence in carrying out their duties.

The actual skill and experience an individual director possesses is often used as a yardstick to determine the standards that are expected of him. For instance, if a director possesses a higher degree of qualifications or skills, he will be judged by how he applies such knowledge and skills.

Duty not to Misuse Powers and Information

Duty not to misuse powers

Directors have a duty not to misuse their powers. As a director, you should be aware that powers conferred by the Articles should only be used for proper purposes and the benefit of the company.

One power that is commonly misused is the power to issue shares, which is normally intended to raise capital.

However, if a director issue shares to dilute a member's shareholdings, gain control of the company, preserve control of the board or prevent a takeover bid, then he has made improper use of his powers as a director.

Duty not to misuse information

The Act specifically states that an officer of a company should not make improper use of any information acquired by virtue of his position. Hence, as a director, you should use such information only for proper purposes and not to profit or benefit yourself or others.

Offences and Effects of Breach

Breach of directors' duties

If a director breaches his duties, he may be subjected to either civil or criminal liabilities, or both. As there is considerable overlap between the common law duties and statutory duties, a breach in a common law duty may also result in a breach in statutory duties. The statutory duties are enforced by a regulator while the common law duties are enforced by the company.

Breach of duty to act honestly

If a director fails to act honestly and with reasonable diligence, he would have breached the common law.

Breach of duty not to make improper use of information

If a director makes improper use of information, he would also have breached the common law. It will result in the following:

(*a*) The director is liable to return to the company any profit made by him or compensate for any damage suffered by the company as a result of the breach.

(*b*) A fine of some amount of rupees or imprisonment for a term not exceeding 1 year.

Breach of duty to disclose potential conflict

If a director fails to disclose potential conflicts of interest in any transaction or due to his holding office, he is subjected to a fine some amount of rupees or imprisonment not exceeding 1 year.

Other offences

Like anyone else, a director must also comply with the general civil and criminal law. If a director steals from a company, upon a police report being made and offences being made out after due investigations, he can be charged with aggravated theft. Another offence would be criminal breach of trust where a director misappropriates company property entrusted to him for his own use. Thus, a director who willfully breaks the criminal laws in the course of his duties can expect to personally face criminal prosecution and all the attendant consequences.

DIRECTORS AND SOCIAL RESPONSIBILITY

Corporate governance is the way in which business corporations are directed and controlled. To quote from the World Bank, "Corporate governance is about promoting corporate fairness, transparency and accountability". There has been an increased emphasis on good corporate governance globally because of the Asian financial crisis in 1997, and also the more recent failures occurring in the Asian and international financial markets.

Corporate Governance

Corporate governance practices may differ from company to company. For instance, smaller companies such as family-run businesses adopt very different practices as compared to large publicly listed companies. This is because listed companies experience the greatest extent of separation between ownership and stakeholders.

Directors of a company are the ones responsible for its governance, and this would include setting the company's goals, providing leadership to achieve the goals and supervising the management of the company. As a director, you are the one in charge, which is why you play an important role in ensuring the good corporate governance of your company.

You should take into account good corporate governance practices when making decisions and setting policies to achieve the following objectives:

(a) Competent leadership by the board

(b) Accountability to shareholders

(c) Transparency in financial reporting

(d) Effective communication with shareholders

The Companies Act can serve as a good guide in this respect, because its provisions were drawn up to steer companies towards adopting proper corporate governance. It is also authoritative because non-compliance with such provisions can result in civil and criminal liability. However, compliance with the legislation alone is not adequate for good corporate governance. The company must on its own initiative seek to adopt best practices other than those set out in the law.

Corporate Social Responsibility

Just as individuals have a duty to be responsible members of the community, companies should also practice Corporate Social Responsibility (CSR). CSR refers to the integration of multi-faceted goals and definitions of success into a company's strategy. Specifically the company should take into consideration and manage the impact of its activities on the environment, stakeholders and the community as a whole, as part of its everyday operations. Public interest and long-term sustainability of a company's presence and activities are thus considered in tandem with economic profit generation, and are often key aspects of risk management and value creation.

There are internationally established tools and guidance principles on CSR. These include the ten principles of the United Nations Global Compact (UNGC), which businesses can become signatories to. The UNGC emphasises four areas: Human Rights, Labour, Environment and Anti-Corruption. The ISO 26000, a non-certifiable standard guide, defines and details areas of Social Responsibility and steps to achieve it. The GRI (Global Reporting Initiative) further provides a platform and tool for organizations to structure their sustainability reports and make incremental improvements on a regular basis.

Being a socially responsible company means following the practices listed below:

Adopting ethical and socially responsible practices

As a director, you should ensure that the company adopts socially responsible practices such as fair employment practices, non-discrimination towards employees and provision of a safe working environment as well as opportunities for employee development. The company should also conduct business ethically and morally by not compromizing on the safety of its products or workers in order to maximise profits.

Ethical practices also extend to corporate governance and transparency, in disclosing a company's actions and transactions in the course of business. This enables a company to be accountable to shareholders and stakeholders, with clear communication channels.

Engaging with society

Aside from donations, CSR entails actual engagement with the community within which a company operates. This encompasses the ethical practices listed above, as well as the environmental concerns elaborated below. Community engagement also includes consideration of cultural and business impacts especially when conducting business in a foreign environment. In particular contexts, this also entails respecting and observing fundamental human rights in all aspects of operations. This helps the company's "license to operate" within the community.

Protection of the environment and sustainable development

The activities undertaken by your company should have minimal or no harmful effects on the environment. The company should continually think of ways to minimise the negative environmental impacts caused by its activities by following good practices such as recycling or reducing wastage.

There are laws which promote CSR such as employment laws and pollution regulations. However, not all aspects of CSR can be legislated. By definition CSR implies a more pro-active stance than mere compliance, and is often a statement of a company's ethical capital. Hence, as a director, you can play a part by ensuring that the company adopts the best practices even if they are not mandated by law.

4

MOTIVATING OTHERS

Motivation is a word that's used quite a lot. Often, it's used in negative terms. You hear about "lack of" motivation much more often than you hear about a person or a group being motivated. "My people aren't motivated," or "My hands are tied when it comes to motivating my people," or "There's nothing I can do to get them motivated" are common management laments. Do today's directors understand that *they* don't motivate people? The truth is, motivation is about what people already want. Everyone wants something. If you can give them what they want, their "motivation" will be satisfied.

Directors need to recognize that they can't make someone want something. Instead, they can determine what people want and provide an environment where those wants can be met. I once set up an experiment with a group of students in a management class. I asked twenty experienced directors to define "motivation." Three of the responses showed a good understanding of this topic. The responses were:

"The drive that makes someone want to accomplish something." "A self-inspired energy that results in a commitment to improve." "The process of accomplishing what one sets out to do." The rest of the responses, however, all referred to things the directors felt they had to do to "get people going." Their assumptions were that they are the active ones in the process and that employees respond to what they do. So, presumably, left on their own without a director taking action, people would be "unmotivated." Some of the responses that showed limited understanding of this topic were:

"Enthusing and encouraging people."

"Keeping employees positive about their jobs and interested in the company's future."

"Praise, inspiration, encouragement."

"The ability to move people to produce more and feel better about it when it is done."

"Keeping them happy."

"Instilling a desire to learn."

"Giving people ambition to perform with a positive attitude."

"Working with employees to get them to work better for me."

"Getting your employees to do their best."

"Convincing others to have great ideas and then effectively execute them."

"Getting them to do the best job possible."

"Be their friend. Be firm but fair. Explain why things happen."

"The ability to get things done through others by instilling a sense of purpose and desire."

"Praising, coaching, and counselling."

The majority of these managers showed they were missing quite a bit. We can construct a simple three-step model of motivation (Figure 1) that illustrates just how self-centred and narrow their responses are. According to this model:

1. A *need* emerges in an individual that creates a sense of deprivation.
2. This need gives rise to tension and creates a *drive.*
3. The person engages in goal-directed behaviour, which involves searching for ways to satisfy the need.

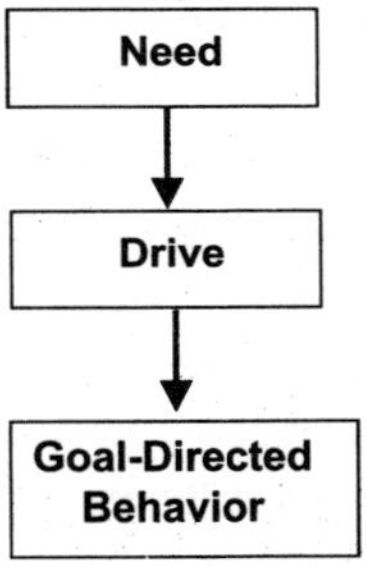

Figure 1. Three-step model of motivation.

How or why that original need emerges no one really knows. And directors shouldn't really care. Do you know, for example, why a certain artist, musician, or dancer wants to work day and night to become the best? You don't and you never will. That person may not know. And it doesn't matter. All you care about is that the person has a strong need. The rest is predictable. So, you don't have to understand anything about the people who work for you or those you work with other than that they need something. If you can provide it, you're in business. You're a "motivator" of people.

We can deduce motives from the way people behave. Motives cannot be observed directly. Thus, we might observe someone attending night classes and infer a motive to achieve. Or someone might like to tell jokes at meetings and we infer a motive to gain attention. Remember, *why* another person has a certain motive should not be our concern. We have enough trouble trying to understand ourselves, let alone trying to understand how others developed their motives. If we're correct in inferring a motive, we then have a means of explaining behaviour. Sometimes the inferences are right and other times they're wrong. If individual employees can tell us directly what they want, so much the better. We can then be in a much better position to try to provide it to them or provide a set of circumstances to help them achieve it.

Developing an achieving workforce that can adapt and has a chance of succeeding in today's fiercely competitive business climate depends on resolving the basic conflict that exists between what is needed to make work productive and what is needed to meet employee needs. Work is theoretically most productive when it is broken down into small jobs that can be repeated over and over again in the same way. This theory was the basis for scientific management and the manufacturing assembly lines introduced during the industrial revolution. Directors, quality control inspectors, and layers of bureaucracy would check people's work to ensure that mistakes were caught. Employees joined unions to protect them from oppressive management practices, and the cost of products kept rising. It was a system that worked for decades. It was assumed that people had to be closely supervised and employee rewards would come in the form of money and benefits.

Trying to have a motivated workforce today requires an entirely different set of conditions. First, the differences among people have to be analysed. People differ with respect to the needs they strive to satisfy. The more directors can match the work with these needs, the more productive people are likely to be. A creative director can find ways to provide for needs such as variety, recognition, sense of achievement, and autonomy in order to achieve both individual satisfaction and high performance.

Directors must be interested in motivation because it's their job to get people to produce a quality effort on organizational goals, whether these goals involve putting tires on automobiles, solving computer programming problems, or granting bank loans that have a high percentage chance of being repaid. Directors in today's organization pay a heavy price for not paying attention to motivation. The price includes conflict with employees, low quality, poor efficiency, absenteeism, and turnover. Motivated employees, on the other hand, contribute creativity, show enthusiasm, strive to not just meet but to exceed goals, inspire their peers to better performance, show commitment to customers, and allow an organization to compete effectively in the global marketplace.

There's a lot directors can do to motivate. But what's most important? What do employees want? Is it recognition? Opportunity to grow? Open two-way communication? You can't give people everything. What's most important to them? What do they feel they're not getting? Furthermore, are there differences between different kinds of employees?

Most experts agree that people want to satisfy some common needs—to make money, to feel important, to enhance self-image, to feel a sense of accomplishment, to work as part of a team, for example. How well these needs are met on the job determines to a large extent how much energy and commitment someone is willing to devote to the job. Ability isn't enough. The highly motivated person often outperforms someone with greater ability. Thomas Edison, regarded by many as the greatest inventor of all time, admitted he had limited ability. He said, "I fail my way to success. I just run more experiments than anyone else." He only slept a few hours a night and just outworked his competitors. In any field, the person with the greatest raw talent is consistently outperformed by those with lesser raw talent but greater commitment to hard work. Of course, the ideal is to have tremendous talent and tremendous commitment to hard work. We call that person a "superstar." They're not just worth 5 percent or 10 per cent more than the average person. They may be worth 500 per cent or 1,000 per cent more. The only problem with these people is that there aren't enough of them to go around.

MATRIX APPROACH TO MOTIVATING PEOPLE

Work is one of the few places where most of people's needs can be met. If management is somehow able to set up conditions so that those needs are met through dedication to critical organizational objectives, you can have something special happen. Look at the top-performing organizations or departments. You'll find that "special something" happening. Sometimes, it's fleeting. It might be a project team that spends a weekend developing something revolutionary. No one can believe the miracles that group performed over the weekend. Sometimes, it's an organization catching lightning in a bottle and showing explosive growth. Other times it's an organization showing steady growth over an extended period of time. Success breeds success. People want to be part of a winning team. When word gets out that your group, department, or company has something special going on, the very best people want to become part of it. Because you attract the best people, the success has a chance of continuing.

The key to all this is directors. They set the group goals, define individual responsibilities, and can provide many of the rewards and incentives that produce high performance. The challenge is that needs and motives can't be seen and can be difficult to measure. Employees can have difficulty articulating what's important to them. Directors then have to infer what drives people. Directors can be wrong in their inferences. Since they can't extensively analyze every person and situation, they should develop practices that motivate most of the people most of the time and establish open lines of communication so they can periodically ask people the following questions:

- What is it that you're getting that you want? (Try to maintain this incentive.)
- What is it you're getting that you don't want? (Try to decrease this disincentive.)
- What is it that you're not getting that you want? (Try to increase this incentive.)
- What is it that you're not getting that you don't want? (Try to maintain this situation.)

The matrix in Figure 2 makes this method easy to remember. Good results are most easily obtained when people's needs are being met. If performance is low, managers should examine how employees' needs are not being met. Threatening people or punishing them typically produces only resentment. Rewards are not always provided for achieving appropriate goals. For example, management typically wants people to set challenging goals and take risks. However, risk-taking is normally seen as something to be avoided since extremely challenging goals are likely to result in failure, which leads to punishment. Most people would rather say, "I met all my goals," even if the goals were quite easy, than say, "I missedmy goals but they were extremely challenging." If you want people to set challenging goals and take risks, it may mean rewarding the person who missed all of her goals when they were extremely challenging more than the person who met all of her goals when the goals were quite easy.

	Want	Don't Want
Getting	Maintain	Decrease
Maintain	Not Getting	Increase

Figure 2. Matrix approach to motivating people.

The first objective of any reward system is to get people to join an organization. Thus, reward systems must, at least, be competitive with those offered by other organizations that you compete with for talent. It is unlikely that qualified candidates would join an organization that offered substantially lower starting salaries, grossly inferior benefits, and little job security. The fact that starting salaries and benefits are quite similar from company to company indicates that organizations pay a lot of attention to these factors.

Once an employee is on board, management is interested in satisfactory job performance. For many organizations, this level of performance is all that is required. If people show up on time and do the minimum required, everyone is satisfied. Reliable work that meets group norms is usually rewarded with predictable salary increases and seniority protection. Whether or not the organization is unionized, it behaves as if it is. In other organizations or with other directors, reliability is not enough.

These directors would like people to perform above minimally acceptable levels. They would like them to solve problems, take initiative, exhibit teamwork, be creative, and contribute beyond their job description. This type of work environment requires rewarding individual achievement that normally results from people getting some intrinsic rewards from the work itself. It requires directors asking their people what's important to them, listening carefully, and then making every attempt to try to give people what they want, as long as it furthers the needs of the organization.

MASLOW'S HIERARCHY OF NEEDS

The psychologist Abraham Maslow developed a theory that has gained wide acceptance as an explanation of human motivation. The key concept in Maslow's theory is that there is a "hierarchy of needs." At the lowest level are our basic biological needs, such as the need for food. Higher-level needs, such as the need to be respected by our peers, come into play as causes of our behaviour only when lower-level needs have been satisfied. Lower-level needs predominate until they are satisfied. Satisfying our lower-level needs renders them inactive, and our attention then shifts to higher-level needs.

Maslow's hierarchy recognizes five distinct levels of human needs, arranged in ascending order (Figure 3).

1. *Survival Needs.* At the lowest level are the basic survival needs, representing a person's need for food, sleep, exercise, shelter, reproduction, and protection from the elements. People are primarily motivated by their biological drives to survive, and they will, therefore, seek work to provide sufficient income for staying alive. When these basic, first-level needs are satisfied, the person is then motivated to work toward the fulfilment of the next higher level of needs.

2. *Safety and Security.* The second level in the hierarchy is the need for safety and security. This is a need to be relatively free from danger and threats and to ensure that the basic survival needs will continue to be met in the future. In today's organizations, some security-related items are life insurance, medical insurance, short-and long-term disability, and workers compenzation. For example, if a person is hurt in an accident, he is very concerned that there be some sort of salary continuance until he is able to return to work.
3. *Social Needs.* The third level is based on an individual's social needs, such as the need to belong, to associate with others, to be accepted by peers, and to give and receive friendship and love. Many social needs are met by associations with coworkers, on and off the job. When these social needs have been adequately satisfied and the person feels accepted, then the next level of needs begins to function as the primary motivator.

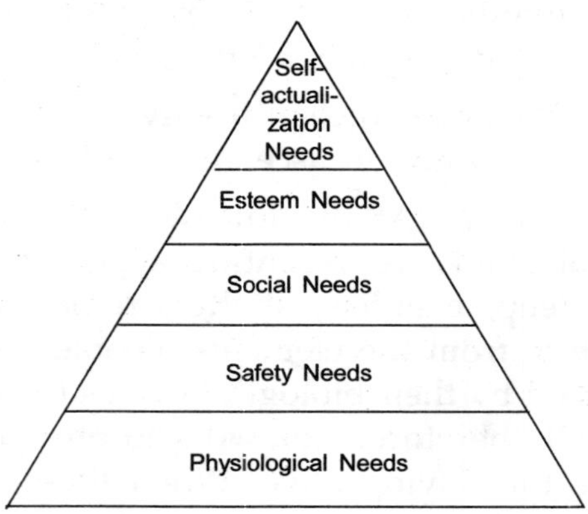

Figure 3. Maslow's Need Hierarchy Model

4. *Ego.* The fourth level of needs—the ego needs—are related to both self-esteem and reputation. The ego

needs related to self-esteem are self-confidence, independence, achievement, and job knowledge. Reputation includes the desire for status, recognition, appreciation, and the deserved respect of peers. When these fourth-level needs are satisfied, only then do the final level needs function as motivators.

5. *Self-Actualization.* The fifth level is the need for self-actualization, or the need to realize one's potential, continually develop and grow, and be creative. In short, these are the needs to become all that a person is capable of being (without joining the army). This highest level of needs is the most difficult to satisfy and tends to be meaningful only for those people who have satisfied their social and ego needs.

HERZBERG'S TWO-FACTOR THEORY

One of the most widely accepted theories of motivation is the "two-factor theory" developed by Frederick Herzberg. He began by asking the question, "Why do people work?" Herzberg observed that people work to meet two very different sets of needs.

Herzberg called the first set of needs "maintenance needs." An individual works to satisfy the basic needs of food, shelter, clothing, security, belonging, and friendship (similar to Maslow's survival needs). The individual needs these things in almost endless amounts and is never quite satisfied with them. When these needs are met, any dissatisfaction that the person may have felt temporarily disappears. But, sooner or later, the need for more food, more clothing, etc., will arise again. These maintenance needs involve essentially the by-products of work. They have little to do with the work itself.

The other set of needs is concerned with the work itself. Long after a person has enough food, clothing, and shelter, he will persist at work, perhaps enjoying it. When asked why, the person might say something like, "It's a challenge," or "I wanted to see if I could do it," or "I've never tried to do anything like that before." If a person's job doesn't satisfy this kind of motivation need, it's likely he will seek some degree of satisfaction outside of work. There are, of course, people who don't strive to meet this need. However, the average person appears to have a need to work that has nothing to do with "maintenance" needs. The motivation need has its roots in the striving for personal growth and achievement.

Herzberg conducted a research project designed to find answers to three questions:

1. What factors cause high levels of motivation?
2. Are the factors that bring about high job satisfaction different from the factors that cause low job satisfaction or dissatisfaction?
3. What happens to people on the job as a result of changed job attitudes?

The data for Herzberg's study was obtained by detailed personal interviews with a sample of 200 engineers and accounting directors from nine companies. The interviewee usually talked about his job, its good and bad points, using specific incidents, for several hours. Regarding the first of the questions, Herzberg found that there were ten major factors that had the most significant effect in causing attitudes to change. They are listed below, in no particular order:

— *Achievement.* Stories involving specific mention of success were put into this category. Examples were successful completion of a job, solving problems, or seeing the results of work. The definition also includes its opposite—failure or the lack of achievement.

- *Recognition.* The major criterion here was some act of recognition felt by the person. The source could be almost anyone—a director, another member of management, a customer, a peer, or subordinates. Some act of notice, praise, or blame (negative recognition) was always involved.
- *Work Itself.* Actually doing the job, or the tasks of the job, was a source of good or bad feelings about it. Events falling into this category were related to the nature of the work and were rewarding, with or without specific achievement or recognition. Examples were creative or challenging work, varied work, or an opportunity to do a job from beginning to end.
- *Responsibility.* Individuals reported deriving satisfaction from being allowed to work without supervision, from being responsible for their own efforts, from being given responsibility for the work of others, and from being given a new kind of job duty. This category also included loss of job satisfaction stemming from a perceived lack of responsibility.
- *Advancement.* This category was used only when there was an actual change in the status or position of the person in the company (i.e., the person was promoted). In situations in which an individual transferred from one part of the company to another without a change in grade level or status but with increased opportunities for responsible work, the change was considered an increase in responsibility but not advancement.
- *Company Policy and Administration.* This category described those events in which some overall

aspect of the company was a factor. There were two kinds of characteristics. One involved the adequacy or inadequacy of company organization and management. For example, there might be a situation where a person was loaned out on projects and received conflicting direction from a number of people. The person might be confused as to who the ''boss'' was. The consequent inefficiency, wasted duplication of effort, or struggle for power would produce frustration. The second kind of characteristic involved the beneficial or harmful effects of company policies. Personnel or financial policies, for example, might be viewed as unfair or may seem to have a detrimental effect.

— *Supervision/Technical.* This category identified events in which the critical characteristics were the competence or incompetence, fairness or unfairness of the director. Statements about the director's willingness or unwillingness to teach would be classified under this category. The principal consideration, however, was how well equipped the director was to answer technical questions about the job.

— *Interpersonal Relations/Supervision.* This category involved the interpersonal relationships that arose when people interacted with their directors in the performance of their jobs. Falling into this category were statements that the director was friendly or unfriendly, honest or dishonest, willing or unwilling to listen, or gave or withheld praise for work done.

— *Salary.* This category included events in which compenzation played a role. Virtually all of these events involved wage or salary increases or unfulfilled expectations of increases. When salary occurred as a factor in low job attitudes, it tended to revolve around unfairness in the administration or perceived inadequacy of the salary increase guidelines rather than the absolute amount of the current salary. Typical problems included increases given grudgingly, increases that were late, a too-small differential between newly hired and experienced employees, and advancement not accompanied by salary increases.

– *Working Conditions.* The final category included stories where the physical conditions of work, the amount of work, or the facilities available for doing the work were mentioned. Adequacy or inadequacy of ventilation, lighting, tools, space, and other environmental characteristics were included. Complaints included inconvenience of the location of the facility, the inadequacy of tools to do the job, and the amount of work required on the job. Interestingly, workers in Herzberg's original study complained of too little work more than they complained of too much work. This is one factor that has likely changed in today's workplace.

Further analysis of the interview data provided an answer to Herzberg's second question: Are the factors that bring about high job satisfaction different from those that cause dissatisfaction or low job satisfaction? There were five factors that were rarely mentioned as producing negative job attitudes. Instead, they were mentioned most frequently when employees spoke of satisfaction with their work. Herzberg called these five factors "satisfiers." In order of frequency, they were:

1. Achievement
2. Recognition
3. Work Itself

4. Responsibility
5. Advancement

The five other factors were rarely mentioned as producing positive job attitudes. They were mentioned most frequently when employees spoke of dissatisfaction with their work. Herzberg called these factors "dissatisfiers." In order of frequency, they were:

1. Company Policy and Administration
2. Supervision/Technical
3. Salary
4. Interpersonal Relations/Supervision
5. Working Conditions

Herzberg further called our attention to a fundamental distinction between these two sets of factors. The "satisfiers" all refer to the job content: achievement of a task, recognition for task achievement, nature of the task, responsibility for the task, and professional growth or advancement in task performance. By contrast, the "dissatisfiers" refer to the job context or job environment: the nature of the company's policies and administrative practices, the type of supervision received when doing the job, the quality of the working conditions under which the job is performed, and the salary received for doing the job.

Since the dissatisfier factors describe essentially the environment and serve primarily to prevent dissatisfaction while having little effect on positive job attitudes, Herzberg referred to them as the "maintenance" factors. The satisfier factors were named the "motivators," since other findings of the study suggested that they were effective in motivating the individual to superior performance and effort.

The third question Herzberg investigated was, What happens to people on the job as a result of changed job attitudes? He looked at three general areas of "effect" and drew the following conclusions.

Performance

- In more than 60 per cent of the cases studied, high attitudes resulted in high performance and low attitudes in low performance.
- Low attitudes toward the job tended to have a greater effect on performance than unfavorable ones.
- When improvement in performance was noted as a result of improved job attitudes, productivity was considerably above standard.

Turnover

- Thirteen per cent of those exhibiting low attitudes quit the company within a year.
- Another 8 percent took steps toward leaving the company. They read help-wanted ads, visited employment agencies, and interviewed with other companies.
- Another 17 per cent said they "thought of leaving" the company.
- Overall, during periods of low job satisfaction, 38 per cent of employees withdrew from the company to some extent.

Attitudes Toward the Company

- During high job satisfaction periods, half of all employees said they had a more favourable attitude toward the company as a whole.
- Low job satisfaction led to a lower regard for the company as a place to work.

- It seems reasonable to conclude that a company may expect the degree of loyalty it gets from its employees to vary as a function of job satisfaction.

Herzberg felt the implications of the study could be summed up as an emphasis on a positive, rather than a negative, approach toward improving the "morale" of people. Few directors are resistant to the need to overcome bad maintenance conditions to avoid turnover, absenteeism, and low productivity. Herzberg didn't recommend eliminating programmes aimed at improving maintenance factors. His finding supported the notion that good maintenance will prevent many of the negative results of low morale.

Yet, good maintenance should only be a beginning. An emphasis on maintenance exclusively means focusing on factors that don't really lead to job satisfaction. He felt the emphasis should be on strengthening the motivators. The rallying cry could be, "Maintenance is not enough!" Motivation to work can be strengthened by an emphasis on greater self-fulfilment. Herzberg only stated this goal and didn't present details on how it could be accomplished.

McClelland's Social Motives

The landmark work of David McClelland on the subject of motivation may be summarized as follows:

- People have a considerable reservoir of potential energy. Studies have not indicated that differences in the total amount of potential energy are important determinants of motivation.
- All adults have a number of basic "motives" or "needs" that can be thought of as valves or outlets that channel and regulate the flow of potential energy from a person's reservoir.

— Although most adults within a given culture have the same set of motives or energy outlets, they differ greatly in the relative strength or "readiness" of various motives. A strong motive may be thought of as a valve or energy outlet that opens easily and has a larger aperture for energy flow, usually due to frequent use. A weak motive can be thought of as a tight valve that, even when open, allows only limited energy flow.

Based on this motivational model, McClelland described three intrinsic motives that have been shown to be important determinants of work-related behaviour:

1. *Need for Achievement.* This is the need for personal accomplishment. A favourite phrase of someone high in this need would be, "I think I can do better." People who have high N-Ach (to use the McClelland shorthand) tend to seek out challenging or competitive situations. They also tend to take moderate risks that are under their control and will set realistic but difficult goals. There are five categories that offer clues to an individual's level of concern for achievement:
   - *Making a Unique Contribution.* The person wants to accomplish something more than an ordinary task or is observed using unique and innovative methods that will lead him to personal success.
   - *Outperforming Others.* The person engages in activities in which winning or outperforming others is a primary concern. Examples are wanting to win a race or wanting to show that you can do a better job or do it faster than others.
   - *Meeting or Surpassing a Self-Imposed Standard of Excellence.* This doesn't involve competition with others but has to do with a self-imposed

standard of high quality performance. Typical examples include wanting to find a better method of doing something, working carefully on a new plan, and wanting to improve past performance.

— *Setting Long-Term Goals.* The mere mention of a goal isn't the basis for assuming N-Ach. There must be evidence of involvement in the long-term goal (i.e., some statement of feelings about or wanting goals that lie years away).

— *Planning to Overcome Personal and Environmental Obstacles.* High achievers carefully plan for the future by trying to anticipate any blocks to achievement of their goals. Evidence of this type of planning can be found in individuals talking about how they have overcome, or have contingency plans to overcome, barriers to goal achievement.

2. *Need for Affiliation.* N-Aff is the motivation to be with others and to share mutual friendship. A favourite phrase of someone high in this need would be, "I really like the people I work with." Concerns of a person with the need for affiliation are:

— *Being Part of a Group or Team.* The individual enjoys being on the "team," sacrifices her own needs for the good of the team, and enjoys the relationships and companionship that group activities can bring. Affiliation activities include parties, reunions, and recreational activities. Important events are baby showers, service anniversary dates, and birthdays.

— *Being Liked and Accepted.* The individual talks about wanting to establish, restore, or maintain a close, warm relationship with others. This relationship is most adequately described as "friendship."

— *Being Involved with People at Work.* The individual talks about people and working with people as the primary focus of work life.

— *Minimizing Conflict.* Steps are taken to avoid disruptions; this person tries to smooth over uncomfortable interpersonal situations.

3. *Need for Influence.* N-Inf (sometimes called the need for power or the need for influence/power) is the motivation to exert influence or control over others. A favourite phrase of someone high in this need would be, "We crushed the competition." This person frequently uses sports and military analogies and expressions. Some clues to a person's level of need for power are:

— *Influencing Others Through Powerful Actions.* Any forceful action serves to express this person's concern for power over others. Examples may include verbal attacks, threats, reprimands, or more subtle actions such as regulating the behaviour of others through policies or giving unsolicited assistance or advice.

— *Arousing Strong Positive or Negative Emotions in Others.* The individual exerts power by causing others to react with emotion to something he has purposely said or done. For a power motive to be indicated, the person's actions or words must provoke strong reactions in others and must be intended to do just that. Simply arousing other people's interest or getting their attention does not indicate a need for power.

— *Acquiring a Reputation or Position.* This individual is concerned with public evaluation (what someone else thinks of her power). The person is concerned about reputation and other people's judgement of her powerful position. Other indicators of the power motive are whether the individual is interested in obtaining indicators of high status or shows disappointment with a perceived inferior social position.

— *Having Control over Situations.* The individual is concerned with controlling people and situations and will seek out positions or circumstances where he can attain this kind of control.

Although any of the three social motives can be found in any organization, you would expect to have many N-Ach people in technical work such as engineering, information technology, accounting, and finance. You would expect to find many N-Aff people in helping positions such as human resources, administration, and customer service. Finally, there would be many N-Inf people in functions such as sales, marketing, and top management. The key to using this theory to your advantage is to identify which social motives are strong in different people and then to design their job to give them what they need.

McGREGOR'S THEORY X AND THEORY Y

According to Douglas McGregor, there are two distinct sets of assumptions about people. The assumptions lead to a consequent approach to management. The first set of assumptions, called Theory X, postulates the following:

— The average person has an inherent dislike for work and will avoid it if at all possible.

— People must be coerced, controlled, directed, and threatened with punishment to get them to put forth adequate effort.

— People prefer to be directed, wish to avoid responsibility, have little ambition, and are motivated primarily by a need for security.

Many of the assumptions in organizations that underlie traditional company rules, policies, procedures, and disciplinary action are based on Theory X. An alternative set of assumptions is called Theory Y. It states the following:

— The expenditure of physical and mental effort in work is as natural as play is to a child.

— People will exercise self-direction and self-control if committed to objectives.

— Commitment to objectives is a function of the rewards associated with their achievement.

— Under proper conditions, people will not only accept but will seek responsibility.

— People want to exercise imagination, ingenuity, and creativity in the solution of organizational problems.

— The intellectual potential of people is typically only partially utilized.

Directors who accept Theory Y push information and responsibility downward. They explain to employees the reasons why things need to be done, ask for ideas and suggestions as to how the job can be done better, and treat people the way they would like to be treated.

SKINNER'S POSITIVE REINFORCEMENT THEORY

B. F. Skinner described how when we do something and are rewarded, we will tend to repeat the act. In other words, the reward acts as a reinforcement. This notion is called operant conditioning, positive reinforcement, or behaviour modification. The key is that by controlling the responses a person gets for his actions, the actions themselves can be controlled. Behaviour modification does not probe into the reasons behind behaviour.

Behaviour modification first developed not as a management theory but as an outgrowth of experiments in psychology labs. These experiments represented a systematic investigation of the observation that behaviour is strongly influenced by factors in the external environment. Pavlov's experiments first popularized the concept of "conditioned response." He demonstrated that when a certain stimulus (such as a bell) was associated with a reflex action (such as the appearance of food, causing a dog to salivate), the stimulus itself could eventually cause the reflex action to take place— the dog would salivate upon hearing the bell.

Skinner further refined the concept of conditioned response by dividing it into two classes—respondent (or classical) conditioning and operant conditioning. Respondent conditioning can be thought of as involuntary, such as the reflexes of Pavlov's dogs. Conversely, operant conditioning consists of voluntary behaviours that are influenced by the consequences that follow and reinforce them. In operant conditioning, all that is required for a subject to perform an action is the subject's estimation that a desired response will occur.

While negative reinforcement and ignoring a behaviour may successfully halt unwanted behaviour, a number of undesirable side effects may be generated. Tension is created under conditions of punishment. The person punished often develops feelings of hostility and aggression. The net effect is usually to make the situation worse. Ignoring a problem causes fewer side effects but has many of the same limitations. It can only control unwanted behaviour and cannot replace it with something more productive. Thus, Skinner felt that positive reinforcement achieves the best long-term results, and behaviour modification programs rely on its use.

Positive reinforcement can take many forms including money, recognition, time off from the job, and praise. In addition, there are several other important ideas related to the concept of reinforcement:

- If one behaviour is asked for and a second behaviour is reinforced, the second behaviour will tend to be repeated. Despite all of the management speeches and policy statements, whatever behaviour is really rewarded will tend to be repeated.
- If behaviour is not useful on the job or has no consequence when it occurs, it will tend to stop occurring. Unrewarded actions are extinguished over time.
- The further removed in time a consequence is from an action, the less effect that consequence will have on the action. Rewards should follow the behaviour closely in order to have full impact as reinforcement.

Positive reinforcement is an ongoing process wherein a director systematically reinforces the positive aspects of the employee's performance. Directors should provide recognition that neither exaggerates nor undervalues the importance of an employee's contributions.

VROOM'S EXPECTANCY THEORY

Originally developed by Victor Vroom, expectancy theory is based on the combination of three variables—effort, performance, and rewards. These variables are defined in the following way:

1. *Effort-performance (E-P) expectancies* are the extent to which the person believes that trying will lead to

high performance.

2. *Performance-reward (P-R) expectancies* are the extent to which a person believes that high performance will lead to desired rewards.
3. *Value of the reward* refers to the attractiveness of the rewards the person receives for performance. This depends, for the most part, on the unsatisfied needs of the individual. In other words, a hundred rupees note might be very important to a homeless person but be seen as something of little value to a millionaire.

Figure 4. Effort, performance, and rewards: expectations and outcomes.

Expectancy theory gives strong consideration to needs, since the performance-reward expectancy depends on meeting important, unsatisfied needs. Expectancy theory points out that motivation is heavily dependent on the actions the director takes. The more the director can do to clarify the two expectancies for employees, the higher their motivation level should be. The attractiveness of the rewards to each person must be considered. For one person, the opportunity to attend conferences and trade shows might be critically important, while for another person it may be seen as a burden.

ADAMS'S EQUITY THEORY

"Equity" is the idea that the value of what a person puts into the job and satisfaction he gets from it are largely determined by comparisons to others. Equity theory, developed by J. Stacy Adams, formalized these relationships. Adams's model says that a person's ratio of job inputs to job outcomes is compared to the ratio for other people in similar situations. When the ratios are about the same, people tend to be satisfied with the rewards they received. When the ratios are different, they usually take action to bring them back into balance. For example, if you feel you aren't being paid enough relative to other people, you might cut back on how hard you work. Or you might start coming in late and leaving early. On the other hand, if you feel you're being overpaid, the resultant guilt might cause you to work harder or longer hours.

There are two important points that follow from these equity ideas. First, relative rewards are as important as their absolute amounts. Second, management must take these equity comparisons into account when giving rewards. This doesn't mean that everyone should get the same rewards. It means that high performance must be consistently rewarded if it is expected to continue. It also means that poor performance shouldn't be rewarded if the high performers are to feel satisfied.

Developing Your Ability to Motivate Others

Demonstrating a focused approach to managing people that emphasizes setting expectations in a compelling manner, measuring and evaluating results, giving feedback, and acknowledging or recognizing appropriate outcomes.

- Demonstrate your personal commitment to the department and your staff and praise commitment demonstrated by them.
- When you assign new projects, take the time to explain how they fit in with overall department objectives. When employees understand how their

work contributes to the whole, their commitment tends to increase.

- Make it a point to regularly reinforce the importance of each person's contributions and the worker's value to overall department objectives.
- Create a high-performance environment where:
  - The focus is clear.
  - The work is challenging.
  - People feel appreciated.
  - Barriers to accomplishing work are kept to a minimum.
  - Resources are available.
  - People help and support each other.
  - Identify your employees' perception of how things can be better tomorrow than they are today. Ask them the following types of questions to gain a clearer understanding of your current environment and what needs to be done to make it more conducive to high performance:
  - What have you done recently that you're most proud of?
  - What gives you the most job satisfaction?
  - What kinds of challenges would you like to take on in the future?
  - What obstacles exist to doing your work?
  - What resources are available to you? What resources are not available that you'd like to have?
- List the needs and corresponding rewards you believe to be most relevant to each employee, based on your knowledge of the person.

— Initiate a discussion with each employee to learn, directly from the source, what that person perceives her needs to be. Compare the list supplied by the employee with the list of your perceptions to determine your level of understanding.

— Observe employees over time and add to or alter the list of needs. For example, you would change the list if you discovered that people did not mention certain needs because they would be embarrassed (e.g., someone might not want to admit that he craves frequent recognition). Conversely, someone might indicate he is interested in advancement even though that's not true. To say otherwise, that person reasons, would be to show lack of ambition.

— Observe employees to determine the optimum timing for rewards. Some employees may respond best to frequent encouragement and recognition throughout a project while others may respond best to receiving rewards upon project completion.

— Seek feedback on your motivational abilities from peers skilled in this area. If appropriate, arrange for coaching to improve your skills. Observe skilled motivators in action and incorporate their approaches.

— Add new tasks to the employee's job to widen the variety of skills used in performing the job. This practice can increase motivation by reducing boredom.

— Increase your employees' authority and accountability. Give them full decision-making responsibility in areas where your approval was formerly required.

— Increase your employees' visibility. For example, an

employee who formerly prepared reports for your signature might now submit them under his own name, or someone who prepared a presentation for you to give might now give the presentation.

— Give employees the opportunity to attend conferences or meetings as the company or department representative.

— Increase the meaningfulness of assigned tasks. An employee who previously completed only a portion of a task might be permitted to handle the entire task alone or with others, to have the satisfaction of producing a total product.

— Increase the amount of feedback on performance. Feedback can come from you or from the employees themselves. For example, a technician can keep a tally of the number of "callback" service calls received on equipment services, conduct a monthly analysis, and recommend actions to be taken.

— Periodically assign special projects that you otherwise would have taken on yourself, to provide challenge and visibility to employees instead.

❖❖❖

5

SELECTING AND RETAINING TALENTED STAFF

A director is the person responsible for managing the affairs of the company and providing it with directions. As a director, you must make decisions objectively, act in the best interest of the company, and be honest and diligent in carrying out your duties. There is no difference between an "active", and "inactive" or "sleeping" director. Under the law, a person is recognised as a director once he has agreed to become one. As such, all directors owe a duty to the company. You have to ensure that the company complies with regulatory requirements, regardless of your level of participation in the company's affairs. Hence, you cannot argue that you are not bound by your director's duty just because you are inactive in the management of the company.

Most employee performance problems can be traced back to the hiring process. When a director points a finger at employees and says, "They didn't work out," most of the time there are three fingers pointing back at the director. The reason is usually "because you should never have hired the person in the first place." The "you" may have been the director before you or the director before that. But a hiring mistake was probably made. Why criticize the employee when we put the wrong person in the wrong job? That doesn't seem fair.

A lot of directors don't give the interviewing process the time and attention it deserves. If you say, "I just need a warm body," then that's probably just what you're going to get (and what you deserve). Bringing aboard a permanent employee is more expensive than most people would imagine.

AVOID COMMON MISTAKES IN STAFF SELECTION

Many directors, unfortunately, select people based on how well they interview. In other words, someone who is glib, articulate, and well prepared tends to be the one who gets the job. Many directors say things like, "I'm very impressed with a candidate who has been on our website and has researched the company." They often say, "I like this candidate because he has five years of experience. The others don't have any more than three." Or they say, "She answered some tough questions very well." You know what? How well someone interviews, how much preparation they've done, or how many years of experience they have is all irrelevant. They aren't useful factors. That doesn't mean, of course, that you want to hire someone who interviews terribly, is totally unprepared, and doesn't have the relevant experience. What you *do* want is someone who has shown a track record of success. Someone who knows how to get things done. Someone who is a good fit for the job. If someone has five years of failing, that's not as good as three years of succeeding on the job.

So, forget if someone is "Our kind of guy" or "Has the right chemistry with me" or "Would fit in well around here." Some of the most successful people I've known, particularly technical people, weren't "our kind of guy" at all and didn't have much "chemistry" and didn't necessarily "fit in well." You wouldn't hire a surgeon to operate on you because he is a nice person, a good corporate citizen, or everyone's friend. You should be hiring people because, based on their track record, there is strong evidence that they will be successful in the job you want them to do.

An effective line of questioning is to ask about "lessons learned." Good people are constantly improving. We take something and make it better. Bad people accept things as they are. For example, if someone conducted a new employee orientation, ask about how he or she improved the programme.

If you're not sure what the key job requirements are, talk to job incumbents. Choose the best people. Make it a focus group of the top performers. They'll help you. It's in their best interest to help. They want you to hire a strong performer because it'll make their job easier. Ask them what the key determinants of success are and what they all have in common. Or simply look at the resumes or applications of the top performers. Compare them with resumes or applications of the bottom performers. Try to figure out what to look for and what to avoid. A little bit of analysis can save you some recruiting nightmares.

It's easy to be impressed with someone who says, "I'm a take-charge person who really responds to a challenge." The key is to use a statement like that as a starting point. It's a good answer but it's a textbook, rehearsed answer. It doesn't mean that the candidate is good. It doesn't mean that the candidate is bad. That's the way most people talk during an interview and they usually are allowed to get away with it. What you need to do next is say, "Can you give me an example of something you really took charge of?" Or maybe, "What was the biggest challenge you've responded to recently?"

Don't ask questions that allow someone to give you theoretical responses. Don't ask things like, "Can you tell me what your strengths and weaknesses are?" or "Can you describe yourself in one word?" or "If you were an animal, what kind of animal would you be?" Instead look for specific examples of what someone has accomplished.

Another useful technique is to ask questions that give negative information. In other words, after asking about a successful experience, ask for a failure experience. You'll typically learn more about a job candidate by the things she tried to do but failed at. You could ask, "Tell me about an idea you sold to management," and then follow it with, "Tell me about an idea you tried to sell to management but couldn't." Don't only use the negative question by itself because it sounds insulting. It's much more tactful to put it after a positive question. You can make a negative question more palatable by doing some self-disclosure.

Typically what directors do is conduct an interview that just covers surface, cosmetic issues. They spread it too thin. They ask vague questions like, "Tell me about yourself?" or "Tell me what you did on your last job?" After a few of these vague questions, the time is up. Guess what? They haven't learned anything useful about the candidate. The most useful thing would be to know if the person is any good. They haven't found that out. A better approach is to limit the focus of the interview to a few projects, work assignments, or accomplishments. Then, dig in with very specific questions to find out what this person tried to do on the job, how he tried to do it, what obstacles he tried to overcome, and how things turned out. You need to continue to drill down until you're satisfied that you have an indication of whether you're dealing with a person who has a track record of success, a track record of failure, or a mixed track record.

If you're interviewing someone fresh out of school, obviously you'll have a more difficult time looking at evidence of accomplishment. Still, there will be things that the outstanding person has done that should point to likelihood of continued success. They've probably overcome obstacles, done volunteer work, held summer jobs, done special projects for professors, or held leadership positions on campus. The advantage of hiring people with no full-time experience is that they come cheaper. The disadvantage is that they certainly are more of a risk, no matter *how* good you are as an interviewer.

SELECT THE BEST

There's nothing more important than surrounding yourself with outstanding people. You owe it to yourself and your organization. Yet, for many directors, it's a bother. They act like it's their lowest priority instead of their highest. The candidates you want are the candidates everyone else wants. You can't always offer them the most money, but you can always treat them better than anyone else. If you've got a 9:00 a.m. appointment with the candidate, show up at 9:00 a.m. sharp, not 9:15. If you tell them that someone else will interview them at 10:00 a.m., make sure that someone else is there. If you tell them you'll get back to them by Friday, get back to them by Friday. There's no excuse for not doing these things. If you're dying, delegate the responsibility to someone when you're still on your deathbed. No excuses. Candidates are watching carefully. Everything you say you're going to do has to get done. If you break commitments during the interview process, people will assume that you'll break commitments on the job. In other words, you can't be trusted.

Try not to ever lose an outstanding candidate. Don't procrastinate. Don't give them the foolish "We're going through the first round of screening and we'll get back to you when we're ready" routine. Jump on them the way one of your salespeople would jump on a purchase order. Don't be afraid to tell them how good they are. Obviously, don't commit to something if you don't have the authority to carry out the commitment. Don't tell the job candidate, "I expect we'll be making you an offer," because you can get into trouble if that person goes back and resigns. Lawyers don't like that kind of thing. But, when you think the job candidates are good, tell them. It's like dating. If you're afraid to tell someone how you feel about them, you have no one to blame but yourself if they go off and marry someone else. At the very least, tell them how impressed you are with their accomplishments.

If you have to have job candidates interview with someone else, set up the appointment on the spot and tell them you'll get back to them to confirm it. That also gives you a chance to "keep them warm." The more times you e-mail or phone them, the better. Just like the way your salespeople deal with prospects. Ask them what other offers they have and get the details about base salary, stock options, bonus arrangement, or other benefits. I don't think I've ever had an applicant who wouldn't give me that information. Ask them straight out, "If we made you an offer, would you accept?" or "Are we your top choice?" or "What concerns do you have about the job?" You might want to have a vice president call the person to indicate how impressed she is with the resume and what good things she has heard about the applicant. Most important, turn things around quickly. If you've got a slow-moving bureaucracy, streamline it. Good people don't last long on the job market. You can't always offer the most money, but you can move faster than anyone else. If the candidate already has other offers, don't neglect to ask her to get back to those companies and ask for more time to make a decision. What do you have to lose? Why *not* ask the candidate to do that? You can be very direct and say, "Would you do me a favour and not accept another offer until we're able to get back to you?" All is fair in love, war, and recruiting.

SELL THE JOB

A lot of directors think they don't have to sell a candidate. They think their company sells itself, or it's the job of the human resources department to sell the candidate. Nothing could be further from the truth. You can't always offer the most money, but you can sell the job the best.

Always be truthful with an applicant. Never exaggerate or withhold information. It doesn't do you, or anyone else, any good for a candidate to say a few weeks or months into the job, "This isn't what I thought it would be." By "selling," we mean putting a positive spin on things. Knowing how to describe the job in an enticing way. Talking about "opportunities" and not "problems." Even if you have the best technical gurus, if they can't represent the company well, you don't want them to be interviewing potential job candidates. You must be able to give a candidate a satisfactory answer to the question, "Why should I come to work for you?" Here are some good ways to sell a job:

- *Use self-disclosure.* This is one instance where talking about yourself is a good thing to do. Talk about why you joined the company, the things you've been able to do there, and what excites you about the job opportunity you are trying to fill. If you can, say something like, "I never thought I'd get the chance to . . . ."
- *Give specifics.* Just like you don't want vague, theoretical answers to your questions, so, too, you

shouldn't give vague, theoretical descriptions of the job opportunity. For example, if an interviewer said, "There's a lot of room for growth here," it wouldn't impress me. Everyone says that. On the other hand, if the interviewer said, "We've promoted 276 people so far this year," that information would definitely impress me. It sounds real.

— *Be a good storyteller.* Talk about specific people and the things they've been able to do at your company. Every organization has had its share of heroes. Know their stories and tell them. They don't have to be members of management, just anyone who has done extraordinary things. If you don't know these stories, do some research.

— *Describe what holders of this particular job have been able to do.* If someone who once held this position is now a vice president, that's a great incentive. Maybe someone in this position won some sort of company award or received a patent or published a paper. Find out real examples of what people have been able to do or how far they've gone.

— *Actually listen to the applicant.* As hard as it is to do, paying attention to other people has its advantages. Ask, "What brings you to the job market?" or "What do you enjoy most about your current job?" or "What career plans have you formulated?" Then take notes or memorize answers. As you describe the job, use the applicant's terminology and phraseology.

— Start sentences with comments such as, "I know you're interested in . . ." and "As you mentioned . . ." and "You indicated that . . . ." Since people aren't used to being listened to, the impact will be significant. Listening is a key skill that salespeople use to build rapport with customers and prospects. We're not talking about pretending to listen; we're talking about being able to quote them. You really have to listen to be able to do that.

— *Talk about successes.* Find out what awards your company and the people in it have won. Describe the "firsts" and the "onlys." Saying that you've got the lowest employee turnover in your industry, for example, is very impressive. People like to be associated with winners. They love to go home and tell a spouse, "You won't believe this but I interviewed with a company that was named the best . . ." or "This company was the first to . . . ."

— *Treat applicants the way you would customers.* Whether they get a job offer or not, all applicants should go away raving about how professionally they have been treated. They'll tell friends, relatives, neighbours, and others in their professional community. An outstanding reputation is built one transaction at a time, just like you build a customer base. For you to get the cream of the crop, the applicants that everyone else wants, you need the best reputation. Then the best will beat a path to your door. The alternative is to have to run big full-page ads in the newspaper, post your jobs on every website, and pay outlandish employment agency fees. Because your reputation is not good, you'll wind up getting the "bottom of the barrel" applicants—the leftovers that no one else wants.

— *Use your top management.* If you tell them you've got a terrific applicant who needs to be sold, my guess is that they'll be delighted to help you. They're used to selling to customers and most of them will do a good job with applicants. Obviously, don't ask a member of top management who wouldn't dazzle an applicant.

If you have a lot of openings in a job category or if you have a single job that is going to be particularly hard to fill, consider creating a DVD to help you promote the job. You can also use employee orientation material, trade show material, or advertising material from your marketing people. Distribute whatever you come up with the same way AOL used to give out CDs to every store in town. If you are trying to fill a position in the IT department, then once you've created your "IT pitch," for example, you can use it for all IT openings for years to come. You can also make an impact by filming interviews with current employees in that job category who can talk about how terrific the job is and the thrill they get coming to work each day. Even if they don't talk that way on a normal day, they will in front of a camera. Don't give them a script, though, but have them talk about the job in their own terms.

Use both your human resources department and employment agencies as an extension of your own department. Bring them into your group and educate them about the work being done in your area. Get them excited about the opportunities you have available. If you have a number of openings, invite every contingency agency from your geographic area, as well as the area of speciality. Put on a show for them. The same kind of show you'd put on at a convention or trade show. Make sure there are giveaways for them to take home. Let them know you want their best applicants and that you expect them only to refer people that they have personally interviewed.

Many directors complain that their human resources department doesn't provide candidates in a timely manner. That's like blaming your accounting department because you didn't negotiate a large enough budget for the coming year. More assertive directors regard HR as simply one of the sources of applicants.

GET THE NEW EMPLOYEE OFF TO A GOOD START

Once new employees come aboard, it's critical that they be made to feel welcome. Be sure someone is there to meet them when they come in and introduce them to others. There's nothing worse than new employees who are treated poorly by "rent-a-cop" security guards packing pistols and attitudes of superiority. New employees don't have badges yet. They're not sure of their new department name. They were told to be there at 8 a.m. and the rent-a-cop tells them their directors don't come in before 9 a.m. They feel like turning around and going home. Make sure the person gets off to a good start. Inform other people in the department whenever new employees are starting so that they don't get greeted with the same questions over and over again: "Who are you?" or "What did you say you'd be doing?" A nice touch is to have announcements with people's backgrounds and personal information about them distributed and posted on bulletin boards ahead of time. If possible, schedule formal orientations for the first week and assign mentors to meet new people at 8 a.m. on their first day, chaperone them around, and take them to lunch.

So, what do you do in your organization for an orientation programme? It's all too common for new employees to be greeted this way: "Oh, hello there. What was your name again? The other people will show you what to do."

RETAINING TOP TALENT

Employees join companies but they leave directors. I've

conducted hundreds of new employee orientation sessions. They are a joy. The newcomers are enthusiastic and have the most positive attitudes you can imagine. They're thrilled about joining such a fine company. I've also conducted hundreds of exit interviews. They are a horror show. Many people on their way out are disillusioned and have the most negative attitudes you can imagine about their director. The departing employee often says, "Look, I'm saying to everyone that there's another opportunity that's too good to turn down, but the truth is I can't wait to get away from my current director. That person has made my life miserable. Just don't repeat that to anyone."

Employee turnover costs money. Lots of it. Concern costs nothing. Obviously, you can't completely eliminate turnover. But if you can cut it down by, say, 10 percent, it would have a dramatic effect on profitability. The key is taking a proactive approach and preventing potential problems. In other words, rather than training people to deal with customers who are angry about late shipments, a better approach is preventing shipments from being late in the first place. If turnover is the issue, directors need to be alert to signals that an employee is demotivated. Instead of ignoring or discounting these signals, a director should act immediately to prevent the employee's concerns from growing into thoughts of defection. Signals to watch for would be a sudden drop in productivity, increased absenteeism, not volunteering for projects or assignments, identifying with or referring to departed employees, withdrawal from the group, being more easily irritated by little things, and talking about burnout.

The interview process can do a lot for someone's ego. If employees are being ignored or taken for granted by their current director, they'll turn somewhere else, and a company interviewing people will roll out the red carpet for them. The hiring director tells the employee that his background is impressive. The employee talks about being underutilized, and the hiring director says, "We'd never do that to you. Someone like you could go a long way in our company." It's enticing. The idea is to never put one of your employees in a position where they would want to interview with another company. Once they do, they're halfway out the door.

When you detect signs that your employees are becoming discouraged, meet with them. Tell them how valuable they are and how much they mean to you and the department. Talk about the signs you've noticed and ask if it's an indicator of their being discouraged. Whatever the employees say, you should listen attentively and try and turn it into actions that you or the employees can take. Always thank them for their honesty and reinforce how important they are to you and the department. Don't just drop the subject. Schedule follow-up meetings. If they deny they're discouraged, that's fine. A little bit of attention can go a long way. At least they know you're interested in them.

What to Do When a Top Performer Resigns

If your preventive measures don't work and people give their resignation, all is not lost. Meet with them immediately. The longer you wait, the more likely you are to really lose them. Assuming you don't want them to go, say something like, "I'm shocked to hear you're considering leaving us after just two years. You're a terrific performer and a key part of our organization. I'd like to ask what prompted you to consider looking elsewhere. If you wouldn't mind, I'd like to know the specifics of your proposed new position. I want to try to do whatever I can to have you stay with us." Don't let them go without a fight.

Hopefully, they'll be open with you and you'll take notes so that you can capture their exact words. Typically, you won't be able to respond to their concerns without talking to your director. So, let them know you'll get back to them quickly. In the meantime, ask them not to tell anyone that they have accepted another offer. The more people they tell, the harder it will be to have them change their mind. Keep saying things like, "Losing a top performer like you would hurt me, the department, and the company. I want to try to provide the same opportunities you're hoping to find at the other company." Even if you're not successful, word will get out that you handled the matter professionally and with a real concern for the employee.

Don't counter-offer with more money. Employees who accept counter-offers are usually gone shortly thereafter because the reasons they decided to look for another job in the first place don't change. The money just delays the inevitable. Besides, once you extend a raise to one employee, you'll have a line of people at your door claiming offers from other companies and threatening to resign if you don't pay them more. They'll figure it's the easiest way to get a raise. That's the wrong message to send. People can always go out and get more money. Dissatisfaction typically stems from problems with the director. That doesn't mean you can pay people in a below-average manner. Pay people well. If certain people are legitimately underpaid, the time to give them equity adjustments is before the fact, not when they have resigned.

A strategy of simply counteroffering with money can backfire. It can cause the employee to conclude: "They just don't get it. Why are they trying to throw money at me now? If I'm that good, they should have offered me that money before. They always cry broke, but all of a sudden they can find thousands of dollars in the budget to try to convince me to stay. It's insulting. No thanks!"

The worst crime you can commit in an organization is to lose an outstanding person. When that happens, there should be a congressional investigation. What went wrong? How could the situation have been prevented? If you worked for me, I'd say, "Make sure it never happens again." And we don't just mean losing people physically, by having them leave the company. You can also lose your employees mentally, by having them withdraw their energy and enthusiasm. In some ways, it's better to lose someone physically. At least you get the chance to replace the worker, hopefully with an outstanding performer. When you lose employees mentally, they may be gone forever.

Characteristics of Outstanding Performers

Outstanding people are strong in at least one of three possible areas. The very best, the cream of the crop, are strong in all three areas:

1. *Motivation.* They work harder than anyone else.
2. *Aptitude.* The work just comes easy to them.
3. *Experience.* They've been in the right places and done the right thing.

Outstanding people can and should be found at every level of the organization. You could feel the energy and enthusiasm the moment you walked into the building. If you dropped a piece of paper, ten people would dive to pick it up. There were signs and banners all over the place. Not the generic type that management buys through mail order, but real signs written by hand by real people. When you're fortunate enough to have outstanding people working for you, you can't treat them like everyone else.

If you don't take care of your special, gifted people, some other company will. Your best performers will think, "I don't get it. I'm doing topflight work and what do I get for it? Nothing. The boss doesn't seem to care. I'm beginning to think management wants mediocrity."

Top performers have three characteristics that are always present:

1. *They have an outstanding reputation.* People come to them for help and advice—both from inside and outside their organization. They've gotten the highest allowable merit increases and bonuses, the biggest stock option grants, and the outstanding performance review ratings.
2. *They produce extraordinary results.* They perform miracles on a regular basis. They somehow find a way to do things they shouldn't be able to do. Ask them about it and they'll give a long history (often beginning with their childhood) of accomplishing things that others thought impossible.
3. *They constantly strive to make improvements.* They're not satisfied with things being "all right" or "good enough." They want to make them better. Because of this characteristic, poor directors may regard them as complainers and malcontents. Look at the most successful entrepreneurs. They all have this drive for improvement.

Extraordinary Directors

So many people spend their time working *in* the business that they don't work on the business. They're involved so closely in the day-to-day workings that they don't take a step back and think about why they do what they do and the impact they have on their work teams. Extraordinary directors point the way. Invariably, everyone will point in different directions. That doesn't mean that the people are bad; it just means they need direction. A leader must say, "This will be our north!" in a convincing fashion. Will the leader be right? Not necessarily. But, without someone taking charge and making the call, people will just argue among themselves or go in opposite directions. A leader always has the right to change direction.

To be an outstanding director, you need a compelling cause. You have to stand for something. Something you can get excited about and, in turn, get others excited about, too. What would your people say your cause is? Some of the best leaders I've known have worked in areas that would seem pretty mundane—payroll, accounts payable, purchasing, and tax accounting. What differentiates them from ordinary directors is that they stand for something special. They want something special for their department. Their cause excites people and attracts the best in their field. You don't want to be "easy" on people. That puts them to sleep. Makes them "brain dead." It's like having a twelve-year-old Little Leaguer only hit off of a tee. That's fine for a five- or six-year-old just learning how to swing a bat, but a twelve-year-old needs a bigger challenge.

Something that you can get passionate about and something your top management will support. Do it today! Your cause has to be something that your people will believe will benefit the organization. They have to believe they are real participants in something seen as important and worth working toward. You must demonstrate your personal commitment through specific actions. Your words aren't enough. It's deeds that count. If you sacrifice for the cause, others will take notice and be more likely to follow your lead. Make sure you keep top management informed and visible in supporting your efforts. People are always keeping an eye on what top management is supporting and participating in.

Gaining Alignment

Your department is like a rowboat and your team members are like the rowers. You want them pulling in the same direction. It's your job to set that direction. You may say, "Things are unsettled now. I need to wait before I set the direction." Bad choice. It's better to set the direction now, based on what you know. You can always change the direction. Without direction, the rowers will all go their own way and fight against each other. They'll churn up a lot of water, but the boat won't go anywhere. Once in a while, unfortunately, you get someone who won't head in the right direction. You've got to say to that person, "We're going this way. If you don't want to come, you have to get off the boat."

What are the differences between those who are aligned on a cause, a vision, a mission, or whatever you want to call it, and those who are not? Here are some:

Those Who Aren't Aligned	*Those Who Are Aligned*
Work for money only	Work foracause
Find satisfaction outside of work	Find satisfaction in the work itself
Just putintheir time	Feel it's important to put in their time and energy
Aren't sure of how their efforts contribute to the organization	Know how their efforts contribute to the or ganization
Describe work in terms of activity	Describe work in terms of outcomes

Make sure you give your people specific goals that will result in the achievement of your cause. One thing I've always done is grade people on "A" goals—that is, those goals that would result directly in achievement of the cause. The "B" goals would be important, too, but more related to the routine day-to-day business. The "C" goals would be those that are worth working on only if time allows. We would generate point values, such as five points for attainment of an "A" goal, three points for a "B" goal, and one point for a "C" goal. There would be a department score each week as well as individual scores. When you make these scores visible, I can almost guarantee you that the results will improve week by week. It becomes like a contest. People are naturally competitive. It's one of the many things that makes work more than "work."

In addition to your employees, there are many others who can help or hinder you in your cause. These people include your director, the person your director works for, your peers, and employees in other departments. These people could provide ideas, information, resources, and other forms of support. You've got to build alliances with them. Go to their staff meetings. Visit them on the job. Have you and your staff constantly evangelize ideas. People forget. They lose focus. They need constant reminders.

On the other hand, there are always people who see will your ideas as threatening the status quo. They're jealous. They're afraid. Sometimes, that person may resist what you want to do because a friend of theirs is resistant to your ideas. You need a plan to deal with those who are likely to oppose your cause. Don't ignore them. Try to include them in planning. Invite them to your staff meetings. I once did a research project on yielding or conforming to groups. We put people in a darkened room and asked them how much a pinpoint of light appeared to move. The actual movement was about one-sixteenth of an inch. Unknown to the subjects, we had some people who were part of the experiment "planted" inside the group to make outrageous claims about the pinpoint of light wavering two or three inches.

As long as we had these people in the group, we could get the other people to see things that weren't there.

Outstanding directors have a positive and hopeful vision of the future. They show how mutual interests can be met through commitment to a common purpose... Someone with true commitment will sacrifice anything for the cause. They're willing to give their all, like a soldier in combat, for the cause.

ACTIONS TO ATTRACT AND RETAIN TALENTED STAFF

Creating a work environment that attracts and retains the best employees with the motivation, aptitude, and experience you want.

- Craft a vision statement for your functional area. Be sure it has the buy-in of your management and your employees. Then "take it on the road" to staff meetings of other departments, community organizations, and local schools and colleges. Typically, the shorter and more dramatic your message, the better.
- Periodically meet with your people to revisit how close or far away you are from making that vision a reality. Each time, do an assessment of past actions and brainstorm ideas for new actions.
- Be sure to "walk the talk." Remember that talk is cheap and intentions are irrelevant. It's actions that count. Plan daily, weekly, monthly, and quarterly actions and then gauge their effectiveness. Remember, the key factor is your enthusiasm and commitment.
- Involve your key people first. Tell the opinion leaders and those that are the experienced technical people that the others look up to them and you'll be relying on them for help. Be sure they're on

your side and will back you up. If not, you may have to ask them to either give you their full commitment or to move on.

— Think of how you should market your message. Why should your customer buy in? What's in it for them? Can you build brand awareness for your inspiring vision of the future? What marketing collateral will you need? It takes more than hats and T-shirts, but they're a start.

— Publicly reward those employees whose actions support your vision and strategic goals. Make them into heroes. On the other hand, if someone has voiced opposition or isn't willing to give you a full commitment, make your expectations clear in writing and don't delay in taking appropriate disciplinary action.

— Look at your entire organization structure and the way work and tasks are organized. If there's a better way, the sooner you improve the structure the better. Be sure new roles are clearly defined.

— Analyze who has succeeded and who hasn't in your area of responsibility. Look for trends. Don't repeat the hiring mistakes made in the past. Also, be sure to understand the hiring successes of the past so that you can repeat them.

— Get your people together to generate ideas on who should be hired and how those people should be recruited. Give everyone the responsibility of ensuring your group is stocked with the best possible talent.

— Similarly, ask your people about your group's orientation process and how it can be improved. You want new people to be "ramped up" in record time. Don't allow someone to be assimilated on a hit-or-miss basis.

— Identify peers who have stocked their organization with top talent. Find out how they've done it.

— Keep a year-round eye out for talent. Even if you have no current openings, it's helpful to know who might be a job candidate should a need arise. If you come across someone outstanding, consider hiring in advance of a need, because it might give you some bench strength. So many departments find themselves in dire straits: "We're swamped. We've got six open requisitions, two people on maternity leave, three on vacation, two out sick. . . ." Try to get ahead of the game. You might consider bringing on temporaries or interns. You might even want to become part of a job rotation programme, so you can "try before you buy."

— Do long-term organizational planning. Cut a requisition well in advance so you'll have plenty of time to search out the best candidate. Recognize that a job you plan to add to your organization four or five years from now could be an internal promotion if you begin preparing someone for it now.

6

MANAGING PERFORMANCE

Organizations try to manage the performance of each employee, team and process and even of the organization itself. Performance management process is very similar, regardless of where it is applied. Every employee can't be a star performer; however, performance management is an essential measurement for employers. Employers establish performance standards that employees must achieve to be considered satisfactory. However, there are times when employee performance drops below the employer's expectations. In these cases, the director must be involved in identifying the problem as well as a resolution to help the employee return to satisfactory performanc

SET REALISTIC PERFORMANCE GOALS

Performance is when an employee is achieving a goal in a highly effective and efficient manner and when that goal is closely aligned with achieving the overall goals of the organization. A common problem for new directors is having no clear, strong sense of whether their employees are high performing or not.

Employees can be very busy in their roles, but that does not mean they are high-performing if their roles are not directly contributing toward achieving the overall goals of the organization. The first step toward solving this problem is to establish clear performance goals. Some people have a strong negative reaction toward setting goals because they fear goals as "the law" that must be maintained and never broken. Some people fear they will never achieve the goals. Others have disdain for goals because goals seem to take the "heart" out of their work.

Despite the negative views that one can have about goals, they hold certain strong advantages in the workplace. They:

- Provide clear direction to directors and employees.
- Form a common frame of reference around which they can effectively communicate.
- Clearly indicate success, and can cultivate a strong sense of fulfilment for those working toward achieving the goals.
- Help clarify the specific expectations of the director and employee.

Goals can be useful for specifying expectations and for setting measurements of progress in working to fill four types of gaps:

Performance Gaps

These gaps are identified during the employee performance management process. Ideally, performance gaps are addressed by performance improvement plans. Performance improvement plans are sometimes a last-ditch effort at helping a person to improve his/her performance. Ideally, the performance problem is addressed through ongoing feedback and adjustments during regular one-on-one meetings. In these plans, goals are established to improve performance, and may include, for example, increased effort on the part of the employee, support from his/her director, and certain training and resources to assist the person in his/her development. Dedicated employees can greatly appreciate having specific performance goals for them to achieve in order to keep their jobs, verify their competence to their director and accomplish overall professional development.

Growth Gaps

These gaps are identified during career planning. Employees perceive certain areas of knowledge and skills that they would like to accomplish in order to qualify for certain future roles and positions. Employees often appreciate having clear-cut goals that mark what they need to do to advance in their careers.

Opportunity Gaps

These gaps are identified when a sudden opportunity arises for the employee. If the person is highly interested in taking advantage of the opportunity, then he or she will appreciate knowing exactly what goals must be achieved to take advantages of the opportunity. Growth gaps and opportunity gaps are very similar.

Training Gaps

These gaps are identified when hiring a new employee, during performance management planning or career planning. Gaps are usually in terms of areas of knowledge, skills or abilities (competencies). Training plans can be designed with clear-cut training goals to give direction to the employee or trainer.Whatever the type of goal, it is critical that the employee have strong ownership and commitment to achieving the goal.

Performance Goals Should Be SMARTER

You can help ensure that goals are agreeable to director and employee by ensuring that they are highly involved in identifying the goals. When setting goals with others, strive to describe them to be "SMARTER." This acronym stands for goals that are:

— *Specific*—For example, a goal to generate three types of financial statements, including cash flow, budget-versus-actual and income statement.

— *Measurable*—For example, to be able to assess if the three types of statements were generated or not.

— *Achievable*—For example, the goal would be irrelevant if the person had no access to the financial information from which to generate the statements.

— *Relevant*—For example, the goal would not be useful if the organization has no plans to ever make decisions based on the financial statements.

— *Timely*—The statements should be generated by a certain deadline, for example, in time for the Board to review and approve the statements.

— *Extending capabilities*—Ideally, the goal involves the person's learning more than they already knew about generating statements.

— *Rewarding*—Ideally, the activities of generating the financial statements would be fulfilling for the person to accomplish. If goals seem insurmountable to the employee, then break goals down into smaller goals, or sub-goals or objectives until they are SMARTER.

SELF-FULFILLING PROPHECY

The term "self-fulfilling prophecy" was first used by Robert Merton and was dealt with extensively in *Social Theory and Social Structure*. Magic was certainly involved in the ancient myth that Ovid told in the tenth book of *Metamorphoses*. According to the story, the sculptor

Pygmalion sought to create an ivory statue of the ideal woman. The result, which he named Galatea, was so beautiful that Pygmalion fell desperately in love with his own creation. He prayed to the goddess Venus to bring Galatea to life. Venus granted him his wish and the couple lived happily ever after. The other name, therefore, for the self-fulfilling prophecy is "the Pygmalion effect."

The London play *Pygmalion,* brought to Broadway as *My Fair Lady,* is the story of Professor Henry Higgins, who insists that he can take a Cockney flower girl and, with some vigorous training, pass her off as a duchess. He succeeds. But a key point lies in the comment by the flower girl, Eliza Doolittle, who says, " . . . the difference between a lady and a flower girl is not how she behaves, but how she's treated." Once she's treated as a lady, Eliza wants to continue to be treated that way. It's very difficult to be treated poorly once you've been treated well.

So much of being an outstanding director involves building people's self-image and capability. A simple truth is:

- *Bad directors* lose the confidence of their people.
- *Good directors* inspire people to have confidence in them.
- *Great directors* inspire people to have confidence in themselves.

The concept of the self-fulfilling prophecy can be summarized in four key principles:

1. We form certain expectations of people or events.
2. We communicate those expectations with various cues.
3. People tend to respond to these cues by adjusting their behaviour to match them.

4. The result is that the original expectation comes true.

It's no accident that some directors complain that their people aren't very good and avoid responsibility. When you talk to those people, you realize the directors are right. Yet there are other directors in similar departments who say their people are particularly good and love to take on responsibility. When you talk to those people, you realize those directors are right, too. Could it be the difference is in the directors, not in the people? That's usually the case.

The simple truth is that almost all of us behave according to the way we're treated. If you keep telling a teenager, for example, that she is worthless and isn't going to amount to anything, it's got to have an impact. On the other hand, if you sincerely and repeatedly tell the teenager that she is wonderful and is going to be a big success at anything she attempts, that has to have an impact, too. Virtually all of us have had a director who believed in us, worked with us, and gave us responsible assignments. We likely responded by doing our best work for that person. In the end, the boss said, "See. I knew it all along." Unfortunately, virtually all of us have had a director who didn't believe in us, criticized us constantly, and didn't give us anything responsible to do. We likely responded by doing our worst work for that person. In the end, that boss too said, "See. I knew it all along."

Directors have a profound impact on the success or failure of employees. Ever wonder why those "high potential" employees do so well when they are brought in? They're often given rotational assignments and special projects. Top management takes a keen interest in these superstars. Guess what? They tend to have very good careers. Were they any better than anyone else? Maybe. Maybe not. It makes you wonder. Is it, "I'll believe it when I see it," or is it really, "I'll see it when I believe it"?

MAKING PEOPLE FEEL IMPORTANT

Making people feel important gives you some real payback. A little over a year ago, a young engineering director told me about a problem he was having with one of his older engineers. He said, "He's got a bad back, so he calls in a lot saying he can't make it in. I try to be nice to him and tell him to take as much time off as he needs. I tell him not to worry about it. We'll cover for him. Take as much time off as you need. But he's out more and more all the time. I don't know what to do." I told the director he was doing it all wrong. "What do you mean?" he asked. I said that the next time the engineer called in complaining about his back, the director should say, "We need you. You're critically important to us. We can't do without you. The customer will want you and no one else to do the installation." He tried that. It's been over a year. The engineer hasn't been out since.

So many directors spend their time trying to make themselves feel important that they neglect spending time on making their people feel important. Some directors (always the worst ones) declare proudly, "I just leave my people alone. I keep out of their way." Ignoring someone invariably produces disastrous results. In fact, in ancient societies when someone was declared a "nonperson" for a serious crime and everyone in a village was required to ignore them, they'd typically waste away and die soon thereafter.

Some directors think a merit increase is a good enough way to show praise and recognition. They're kidding themselves. All employees know, either through official or unofficial channels, what the merit guidelines will be. If they figure they'll be getting about a 4 per cent raise and that's what they get, they're satisfied. If they get less than that, they're angry. It's rare that they wind up getting more than they expect. So, for most people, the merit increase is a nonevent. It amounts to a few extra money that they've probably already spent. Especially if it's given in the usual cavalier manner in a performance review after the director humiliates them with a bunch of grade-school talk about "work habits" and "citizenship" and "attitude."

The good news is that you'll always have an unlimited budget for praise and recognition. No one can ever take that away from you. An occasional "thank you" goes a long way. But there's something that's even better than a "thank you." What really has a positive effect is a token of appreciation. Something people can touch, feel, hold in their hand, and show to others.

A director should be just as alert to what interests a person as a salesman is to what interests a prospect. If someone talks about their golf game all the time, maybe a set of golf balls would be a nice token of appreciation. If they mention they didn't bring an umbrella to work on a rainy day because they lost theirs, a new umbrella would be a nice token of appreciation. If you don't know the person very well, a quick call to a spouse or a significant other might yield some clues as to what would give them a "charge." It's also awfully nice to say to the spouse something like, "Your husband has really done a terrific job on the big project. We'd like to thank him in some small way." That's like getting double mileage.

IMPORTANCE OF COACHING

By recognizing accomplishments, outstanding directors encourage people to persist in their efforts. These directors have extremely high expectations of people and teams and let people know that their efforts are appreciated. Any leader in any field of human endeavour says to people, "Come on. You can do it." They believe in people so much that the people begin to believe in themselves. Imagine if a sports coach behaved like too many directors do in a work situation. If a track athlete stumbled and fell, the coach would come over and say, "Look, I told you to run fast. What's wrong with you? Why didn't you listen to me? I'm going to keep my eye on you." But that doesn't happen because both the athlete and the coach know that the coach exists for one reason and one reason only—to help the athlete succeed. The track coach would run to the fallen athlete and say, "Are you all right?" The athlete would probably say, "Coach, I let you down. I lost the race. You worked so hard and believed in me so much. I'm sorry." We all know the coach would say to her, "It's okay. There'll be other races. Let me help you up. We'll start working on the next race right away."

So, ask yourself: What did you do the last time an employee asked you for specific performance feedback? What did you do the last time an employee made a mistake?

Coaches aren't confused as to whether they're a coach or an athlete. They are mature enough to recognize they have to remain on the sidelines. Imagine a football coach who went on the field of play because it was "crunch time." He might say to the field goal kicker, "This is too important. I'm going to make the field goal." Talk about discouraging someone. The poor player would say, "I get it. Whenever it's important, the coach pushes me off the field and takes over."

There are too many "field goal kickers" around organizations who know they're going to get "pushed off the field" because the director loves to take over difficult situations. That would never happen in the world of sports. The football coach would be fined and maybe suspended for venturing onto the field of play. I propose we fine directors who do work that their people should be doing. Everyone who is promoted to director should sign a document saying, "It's not about you anymore. The employees are the ones who are going to get the gold medals and get their pictures on the covers of the magazine. Get it? Don't mess up your team by trying to be the hero."

SKILL OF LISTENING

Begin really listening to employees on your first day of work, and do it every day thereafter. Real listening is not just waiting for your turn to talk. It's understanding the *meaning* of what someone is trying to say. People always communicate at two levels—what they say and what they mean. "What they say" is the level most directors pay attention to, if they pay attention at all. For instance, the employee says, "Congratulations on the promotion. I know you worked *so* hard to get it." Unfortunately, the comment is dripping with sarcasm.

The director is totally oblivious to the real meaning and says, "Thank you." Or I ask my wife what's wrong and she says in an angry tone, "Nothing!" Or I ask someone how their project is going and they say dejectedly, "Oh, just great!" Real listening is paying attention to the subtext, to the vocal element of the way something is said, and to nonverbals. It's a lot to ask of someone to actually listen, but it's a great opportunity for a director who wants to be better. What's the number-one answer I get when I ask employees what their director could do better? You got it. It's listening.

In this sense, employees are like customers. They deserve to be treated with respect. The number-one way to treat people with respect is to listen to what they have to say. You can't always give them what they want. But you can always listen to them. Directors are often unskilled communicators, particularly when listening is involved. They fail to ask simple, com-monsense questions such as, "What do you think?" or "Does this make sense to you?" or "How do you think it should be done?"

Why are people so bad at listening? I've got to believe it's the way we're brought up. The other communication skills are talking, reading, and writing. Think of how young we are when we're taught those things and how many years in school we have of emphasizing those things. That isn't to say people shouldn't be taught to be better talkers, readers, or writers. Yet, when are people taught to listen? How many years in school do we have of emphasizing it? The answer is that people aren't taught to listen, and there is virtually no instruction in listening. We also don't learn good listening skills from our directors because the odds are they aren't good listeners. I've got to believe that listening is the forgotten skill. Here are a few tips for becoming a better listener:

- Don't multitask. If you are going to listen, then listen. Give the person your undivided attention.
- If you're busy or distracted, tell the other person that it isn't a good time and reschedule the meeting.
- Take notes. It shows the other person you're taking them seriously and helps you recall the converzation.
- Periodically summarize what the other person is saying to you. It teaches you to listen and checks your comprehension.
- Try to be open-minded and not anticipate what the other person is going to say.
- Pay attention to the way someone says something and to the other person's nonverbals. Dr. Albert

> Mehrabian, in his book, *Silent Messages,* divided communication into three components. He found that the verbal element (the words) accounted for only 7 per cent of the meaning, whereas the vocal element (the way the words are said) accounted for 38 per cent of the meaning and the nonverbal or visual element (the body language) accounted for 55 per cent of the meaning. No wonder e-mail is such a limited form of communication. It's great for confirming agreements and follow-up, but terrible for topics that are controversial or have strong emotions involved.

The director thinks she has done a great job and the employee vows never to bring up an issue with the director again. It's insulting and demeaning to be told what to do when the person doesn't even understand the issue

KEEPING DISCUSSIONS POSITIVE

One of the important things that outstanding directors do is get their people to focus on positive things. Too many groups spend too much time complaining about things they can't do anything about. They lose focus. As a leader, you need to have strong conviction that you want time and energy spent in a useful way. You must express that to your people as often as necessary, saying in no uncertain terms things like, "Look, we've got a lot of work to do. We're not going to waste time talking about that." You set the ground rules. That's your job.

Figure 1 is a classic diagram (usually called the "locus of control") that illustrates what I'm talking about. Just like in baseball before the game, you review what's in bounds and out of bounds. When something is out of bounds, you have to be like an umpire and shout "Foul!" Things in the inner circle—"what we can control"—are always suitable topics.

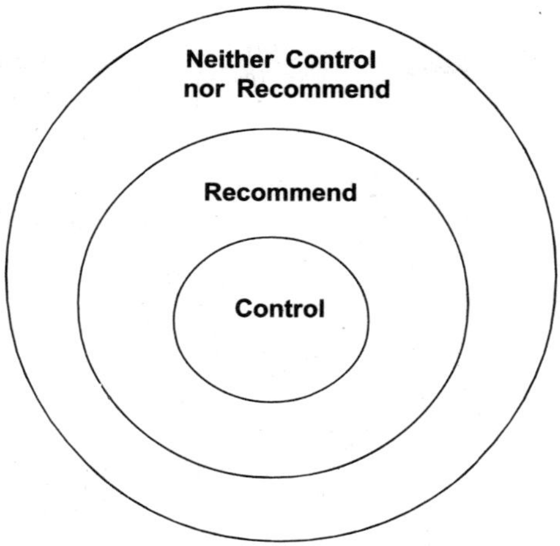

Figure 1. Locus of control

You and your people want to discuss methods and process improvements constantly. Tell your employees to bring up these issues in meetings or one-on-one with you. These are things that you can authorize on your own without getting anyone else's permission. Things in the middle circle—"what we can recommend"—may be suitable topics. These are new policies and procedures or changes to existing ones. Typically, you would encourage people to bring these issues to you and then you'd decide whether it's worth pursuing with those you work for or those in other organizations. Things in the outermost circle—"what we can neither control nor recommend"—are taboo. They're not a good use of anyone's time.

IMPORTANCE OF DELEGATION

Delegation is the transfer of responsibility for a specific task from you to one of your employees. It can either be a one-time or a continuing responsibility. This means that you'll depend on the employee to handle that task and meet the required performance standards. Sounds easy, doesn't it? It isn't! When you delegate, you must make sure the employee thoroughly understands the new responsibility and has the knowledge and ability to successfully handle the new task.

For instance, many parents have had the experience of teaching a child to ride a bike. You can't progress too fast. You hold the handlebars, put on training wheels, and walk alongside the bike. A child typically will say, "You won't let go, will you?" You say, "Of course not. Not until you're ready." Delegation has to be done the same way. You've got to hold the handlebars, put on training wheels, and walk alongside the bike while your employees learn to ride. It is irresponsible for you to just push them down the hill before they're ready. They'll crash and you'll be to blame.

Often, we just take for granted that the other person understands what we want. Let's use another example of a child. You tell your child to go and clean her room, but she gets distracted. You say, "That's it! Get up there now! I'm coming up to inspect and that room had better be clean!" After a minute or two of cleaning, the child says, "Okay, I'm done." No way," you scream, "You couldn't have done it that quickly." The child insists that she has. You go upstairs to inspect and bellow, "You call this clean? This isn't clean. You lied to me!" The child starts to cry and says, "I did, too, clean it." What's the issue here? You never defined specifically what you wanted. You just assumed the child knew what a "clean room" was. It's likely you never gave the child a checklist or detailed explanation of what you expected. That happens in your organization every day. People assume that others know what they have in mind. They might ask, "Do you understand?" People typically say "Yes!" whether they really understand or not. They don't want to look stupid. A better thing to ask would be, "Can you give me a detailed explanation of what you're going to do?"

What's in it for you to delegate?

- *You can devote more time to important management matters because some of your other functions will be handled by your employees.* Most directors feel that they don't have enough time to perform all their job functions. By delegating work, you'll be able to devote more time to those matters that require your attention.
- *You can challenge and motivate employees.* Many talented employees feel underutilized. Assigning challenging responsibilities to them will often bring about increased interest in the job. Many times, these employees show enthusiasm and ability that previously had not been apparent.
- *You can develop employees and make them more valuable.* Additional responsibility may increase an employee's value. New job responsibilities provide additional job experience and training and enable the employee to contribute more. Just feeling more valuable to the organization can be motivating.

There are some clues that can lead you to ideas for things you can delegate.

Getting Employee Commitment

A good way to get delegation ideas is directly from your employees. Certainly if they can ask for something, they're much more likely to receive an assignment in a positive frame of mind. The ideal way to delegate is to be able to say something like, "You mentioned that you wanted to get more visibility with top management. I've got a project that will do just that for you." Much better than saying, "I'd like to have you do this project for me."

We've all rented cars before. No one has ever changed the oil, done a tune-up, or rotated the tires on a rental. Why? There's no ownership involved. It's someone else's car. While there's no guarantee, there's certainly a greater likelihood that you'll take care of your own car. You want to make assignments that give employees a feeling of complete responsibility and not just a feeling that they're doing a task for you.

You also want them to use their ingenuity. So many directors get hung up on the fact that they might have more experience or technical know-how, or they think they're smarter than the people who work for them. They think they can do it better. That's only half of the equation, though. Let's say you can do something that's a 94 on a 100-point scale of being right, and your employee can do it only at an 84 level. It might appear that you should have the person do it your way. But, in addition to the rightness of the decision, there's a second consideration called "commitment." Your 94 could be multiplied by, say, 10 per cent in employee commitment. Letting someone do it their way at 84 could be multiplied by a 90 per cent in commitment.

Both rightness and commitment carry equal weight. But look at Table 1.

Rightness	*Commitment*	*Result*
94	10%	940
84	90%	7,560
100	0%	0
0	100%	0

Table 1. Balancing rightness and commitment.

Letting someone who has the ability do it their way is usually a better deal. You don't have to know much about math to know that if something is done totally wrong with 100 per cent commitment, the product result will be zero. On the other hand, even if something is 100 per cent right and there's zero commitment, you'll get a zero result in the end. That's why it's common to see great ideas fail and mediocre ideas succeed. Commitment is a key ingredient. So, what's the lesson? Be very specific on the end results needed. Make sure your employees understand them. But, if it's at all possible, let them come up with the way to get the task accomplished.

THE RELUCTANT EMPLOYEE

When an employee is asked to accept a new responsibility, he may want to think it over before giving you a commitment. It's not unusual for someone to say, "I'm sorry, but I can't do that. I've never done anything like it before. No thanks." Then, the person comes back the next day and says, "You know, I've been thinking about it. That thing you wanted me to do. It would be a real challenge. I was scared off at first. Is it still available?" This is likely to happen if the new responsibility seems extremely challenging or the employee feels he already has too much to do. You may pay a price in lack of commitment if you force the responsibility on the employee. Instead, ask the employee to think it over and agree on a specific time when the two of you can meet again to discuss the task. Be sure to emphasize the reasons you're asking the employee to take on the new responsibility.

It's often helpful to remind employees of challenges met and new responsibilities they have successfully taken on in the past. If necessary, you can ask employees to do you a favour and take on the new responsibility because it would mean a lot to you and the organization. Be sure to express appreciation now, and again later, for their willingness to help out.

If people are reluctant to take on new assignments, it really helps if you tell them why you're choosing them for the assignment and can review their recent accomplishments. For instance, if you can say, "I'm asking you to do this because you're the best we've got at negotiating agreements," that kind of sincere flattery goes a long way. Don't make it up. It's got to be real. Then follow up with a specific example, if possible: "You were the one who took on that extremely difficult Alpha project. No one thought you'd be able to pull it off, yet you did. And how about the work you did on Beta? That was amazing." You can and should make it awfully difficult for someone to say "No" to you. Do it through praise and specific facts. Don't ever do it through threats or intimidation.

KEY ISSUES

There are four key issues to ask when giving someone a work assignment. Most directors, interestingly enough, ask none of the four questions:

1. *Will you do it?* Amazingly, most directors just say, "Here's what I want you to do," or "Do me a favour," and they never ask for a commitment. To significantly increase the likelihood that the person will actually do what you're asking, get the person to say out loud that she will do it. Don't just assume she will. Also, if the employee says something like, "I'll try. A good director says: "There is no try. There is only do. Do or not do." So, don't accept any "maybes."
2. *How will you do it?* It's one thing to agree you're going to do something and quite another to put together a plan on how you're going to accomplish it. A good director will always ask for an action plan. Many directors have foolish, worthless converzations. "I need you to cut down on your errors," the director will say. The employee says, "Okay, I'll try to do better." The director says,

"Good. I'm glad we had this little talk." That talk was worth nothing. A smarter director will say, "What exactly are you going to do differently?"

3. *What could prevent you from doing it?* Excuses after the fact aren't worth anything. But, before the fact, they're very useful. Ask the employee all the things that could go wrong. If he doesn't know, have him talk to those who have worked on similar projects or assignments. Have employees give you all the excuses for failure before they even start on the task.
4. *What could you do to overcome that problem?* For each of the excuses, have employees think through what they could do to take preventive action. If the preventive action doesn't work, then ask them what they could do to get back on track.

The best directors are devoted to two things—meeting the needs of the organization and meeting the needs of their employees. To do just one of these things is not being a complete director. To do neither one of these things puts you in the category of taking up space and not really having any added value. To do both of these things makes you invaluable to your organization. You're never done with the effort since the needs of the organization and the needs of its employees are constantly changing. But, if you're good, you walk the tightrope and somehow never fall off.

TIME MANAGEMENT

Your life is crazy, isn't it? It's getting crazier all the time. Just too much to do and too little time to do it. Your personal life is just like your work life. It's a roller-coaster. It's always been that way, but it seems the roller-coaster is getting steeper, the curves more and more frequent, and there aren't any more straightaways where you can relax. Well, you're not alone.

You've got to come to grips with the fact that you can't get it all done. You can't be all things to all people. If you try, you'll be like a juggler attempting to juggle forty-seven balls in the air at the same time. You'll drop them all. You'll never be praised and rewarded for attempting to do many things. You'll only be praised and rewarded for what you successfully complete. So, concentrate on the few important things. Get them accomplished.

Remember the discipline you had in school? You'd always want to know if something was going to be on the exam. If so, you'd study it. If not, you learned to let it go. Work is just like that. If it's important, do it. If not, let it go. There are too many people who go around saying, "I can't get to the big, important things because the little day-to-day things keep getting in the way." It takes courage to say, "Wait a minute. It's the big, important things that matter. I should do them first. If I have time left over, then I should do the little day-to-day things." Why don't people work that way? They're afraid. Afraid of getting in trouble. Ironically, because they do the little things first and don't get to the big things, they *do* get in trouble. They spend their time on tasks inversely related to their importance. People exhibit a lot of characteristics at work. Unfortunately, courage is not usually one of them.

We've got all kinds of electronic gadgets to help us become better organized. Unfortunately, they often add more clutter to our already-cluttered lives. These things may help us to be more efficient, but they don't address the real issue—*efficient doing what?* We need to take a penetrating look at how we spend our time instead of just saving it to waste it again.

Here's a four-step process that every director at every level in every organization should follow.

1. *Concentrate on what's important.* Decide on what's meaningful and eliminate the distractions that keep you from pursuing it. An obvious point, yes, but most of us fail to do it. Instead, we busy ourselves with trivia. A good rule of thumb is to stop doing the unimportant things you have time to do and start doing the few important things you don't have time to do.

2. *Question everything you do.* How much of your job is devoted to ritual and routine tasks that are of questionable importance? If you find yourself working harder and getting less and less done, this may be at least part of the problem. Stripping away these extraneous things can be a pain ful process. It takes clear thinking and relentless hard work. It's kind of like cleaning out the attic. If you don't need it, get rid of it! Keep asking why you have to do something until you discover if a specific task is necessary. Unless you're willing to keep going until you find an answer, you'll keep performing activities rather than producing results.

   How many bureaucratic procedures, reports, meetings, and other activities go on in your department because you've "always done them that way." Question them all. Once you're done, question them again. Get in the habit of thinking like an outsider and looking at your job as if you're seeing it for the first time. Something that was appropriate one month may be inappropriate the next. Constantly ask yourself and your staff what tasks could be pruned. If you must add a procedure, meeting, or new task, try to take an old one away. Everyone knows it's good to have a to-do list of activities each day. It's probably better to have a not-to-do list of activities each day.

3. *Stop time-robbers.* The chief duties of many directors involve nothing more than completing plans, communicating results, reporting on why results did not meet plans, reporting on why results did meet plans, summarizing results, and summarizing summaries. How useful are these activities? Or, rather, how much do these activities cost the organization? Isn't it interesting that when a company eliminates layers and layers of management, its stock price immediately shoots up. Wall Street is smart. A little less bureaucracy is good for an organization. Wall Street knows that the role of too many directors has become one of trying to please those they work for and irritating those who work for them.

   These directors surround themselves—suffocate themselves—with electronics that are attached to and hanging off their bodies like parasites. They talk into invisible microphones. Some of them boast proudly of the thousand e-mails they get each day and how they have no time to open them, let alone read them. They go from one conference call to another. They're so addicted to their BlackBerrys that they might as well be called "CrackBerrys." They multitask themselves, and their departments, to an early grave. Thoreau was a prophet when he said: "Men have become the tools of their tools. . . . Our inventions are wont to be pretty toys, which distract our attention from serious things."

4. *Don't ask permission.* Anyone at any level can make positive change. Unfortunately, many people feel they don't have the authority to make those changes. The idea of taking action is frightening to

> many directors. It takes courage. How many acts of courage do you see in your organization in a typical day? Probably not enough. People also love to say, "It's got to start at the top." What exactly has to start at the top? "If I'm going to improve my effectiveness, it's got to start at the top," the director says.

Very few people ever get in trouble for becoming more effective and productive. Be a role model for everyone else. Get outstanding performance reviews. That's the only real protection you'll ever have. Become invaluable to your organization. Then you've got the autonomy you need. Don't be run by the mindless bureaucracy, because then you'll be part of the problem and not part of the solution.

This is the kind of mental toughness that Thoreau was suggesting when he wrote: "No way of thinking or doing, however ancient, can be trusted without proof. What everybody echoes or in silence endorses as true today may turn out to be falsehood tomorrow, mere smoke of opinion. . . . Old deeds for old people, and new deeds for new."

The Work-Planning Pyramid

Approach time management the way you would any business issue. It's all about coming up with a plan and then executing the plan. When things take you off course, either get back on plan or revise your plan. Start big and then work your way down the "work-planning pyramid" as illustrated in Figure 2.

Start with your vision of what you want to accomplish by the end of the week, month, year, and lifetime. You can't decide how to get somewhere if you don't know where you're going. Your personal vision can change from time to time. No problem. Then, plan on the goals that will help make that vision a reality.

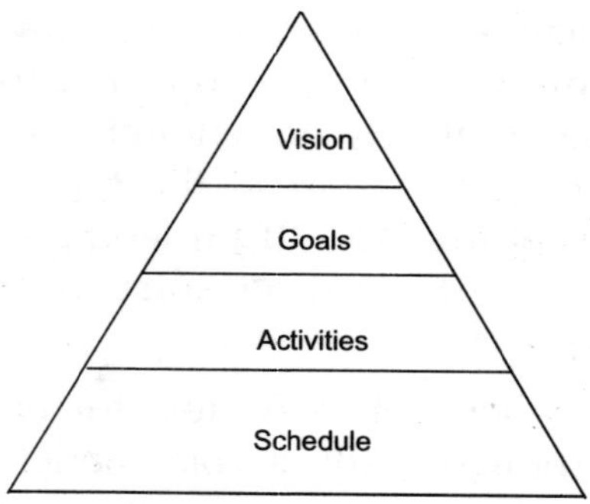

Figure 2. Work-planning pyramid

Every goal should be divided into short-term activities. It may take a hundred activities to accomplish one of your goals. Each of the activities will take time, so you need to schedule them in. Too much work? You know the old expression, "If you fail to plan, you're planning to fail." What's your choice? To be driven by events? Wouldn't you rather drive events? See what happens? Play it by ear? Those aren't the things that take-charge people say. It's doubly tough on you. As a director, you have to be terrific at the difficult things we're talking about and then also teach your people to do them. The best way to teach, of course, is to be a role model. Teach by your actions.

Time-Management Matrix

So, what's the best use of your time? Let's take a look at the time-management matrix in Figure 3.

Most people's jobs are dominated by Quadrant I activities—those activities that are important and seem nondiscretionary. You "have to do" the fire-fighting. You are stressed by deadline-driven projects and consumed by problems, and you handle one crisis after another. Right? That's what everyone around you is doing. That's your "culture." The problem with only doing Quadrant I activities is that they're reactive. You respond to issues. It's kind of like shoveling sand against the tide. You work hard, but you don't really get anywhere.

	Nondiscretionary	Discretionary
Important	I Fire-fighting Deadline-driven projects Problems Crises	II Relationship building Process improvement Planning Coaching and developing others
Not Important	III Phone calls Meetings E-mail Drop-in visitors	IV "Retained hobbies" Passing information Bureaucracy Monkeys

Figure 3. Time-management matrix.

The way to cut into Quadrant I is to invest in Quadrant II activities. They are also important, but they're discretionary, so most people don't spend much time on them. Some directors spend no time on them at all. They include building relationships, implementing process improvement so things are made easier, planning, and coaching and developing others. These are proactive activities. You invest in these activities. They pay off later for you. That's why people put off doing them.

Quadrant III activities seem nondiscretionary, but the key is that you define them as nonimportant or, at least, of lesser importance. You have to deal with certain phone calls, meetings, e-mail, and drop-in visitors. You can't ever eliminate these things entirely. But you can spend less time on them. For example, you're asked to give a fifteen-minute presentation as part of a two-hour meeting. Most people will sit through the entire two hours. Maybe they'll get to you. Often, they won't and you'll have to come back next time. A good time director will say, "Could we do my presentation for the first fifteen minutes? I'd appreciate that." Some of the time, at least, the meeting planner will say, "Sure, no problem." That's the kind of thing I'm talking about. A little thing that can potentially save you a lot of time.

Quadrant IV activities are the most interesting of them all. They're discretionary and unimportant. You'd think people would never do them. But some people are overwhelmed by them. They're things like "retained hobbies," passing information, dealing with bureaucracy, and "monkeys."

ACTION PLANS FOR IMPROVING YOUR GROUP'S PERFORMANCE

Defining, organizing, and scheduling work requirements in order to appropriately assign tasks, secure commitment, allocate resources, and monitor progress toward desired outcomes.

- Get clarity from your director on what the specific expectations are for you and your department for the coming quarter, six months, and year, so that you can focus your efforts appropriately. Ask for performance targets that have quantitative measures.
- Together with those who assign you work, develop a method for sorting requests according to their priority. After using the method for a while, check back to make any needed changes.
- Before starting a task or assignment, ask yourself what could go wrong. Plan and take steps to prevent potential problems.
- Break-down larger activities into smaller, more manageable steps. Set milestones and deadlines for

each step to keep yourself on track and to help mark each accomplishment that moves you closer to the achievement of your larger goals.

- Be able to define how your work is measured and assessed. Make sure your definitions are in line with those of your director.
- Determine ahead of time a way to reward yourself for accomplishing a key goal or objective (e.g., decide that you will have lunch at a good restaurant).
- Ask your director to explain the broader business context of a project or assignment so that you know how what you are being asked to do contributes to the company's overall business objectives. Use this knowledge to determine how you'll measure the outcome of your work.
- Take courses in time management, project management, and project planning to learn about tools and techniques you can use to schedule, organize, and prioritize your work effectively.
- Learn about and use existing resources (e.g., people, tools, systems, processes) that can help you track and measure your progress on projects and assignments.
- When developing project plans, take into consideration your other work commitments. Map out a timetable and set expectations that are challenging but realistic and achievable, given other work obligations or project demands.
- Set goals with short-term steps to give yourself a sense of achievement as you work toward accomplishing the bigger and broader objectives.
- Develop a time-management system that is flexible enough to allow you to reprioritize your work as

demands change, so your attention remains focused on accomplishing the most important activities first.

— Observe peers in other work groups who are known for getting results. Note what processes and/or systems they use and adopt those that seem appropriate for your department or work group.

— At the beginning of the week or month, choose an issue that has been causing you frustration and that you've been meaning to address. Plan and write out what steps you'll take to move it to resolution.

❖❖❖

7

DRIVING FOR RESULTS

Driving results in an organization requires more than just a personal best effort. Rather, positive organizational results come from the coordinated effort of many people. Leaders who consistently obtain high levels of performance and effectiveness from their organizations identify and focus on goals and objectives that are truly important to the organization. They assume personal responsibility for organizational achievement, challenge others to do the same, and persist despite obstacles.

As you might guess, it would be impossible to provide a comprehensive primer in just a few pages. Many books have been written on this topic. Below, we try to provide you a general overview of the most important issues.

IDENTIFY THE TARGET

There will always be many demands upon the resources of your part of the organization. To be effective, you must sort out the truly important from the potentially distracting. You must define for yourself and your group those results you wish to obtain above all else, and you must clearly and consistently communicate these objectives to your group. As you define these objectives, remember that good goals are:

- *Specific.* Set goals that are specific rather than general. For example, a specific goal like "increase production by 10%" is more effective than a general goal like "do your best."
- *Public.* Everyone in the organization should know and understand the goal, key milestones and progress to attainment.
- *Participative.* People are more likely to adopt goals as their own if they have participated in the goal setting process.
- *Challenging, but attainable.* In general, higher goals lead to higher results. However, people must believe the goal is attainable or they will not commit to it.
- *Measurable.* Progress to goal achievement should be measurable by objective standards and regular progress feedback should be available to all people involved. Progress feedback is an important motivator for most people and will reinforce the achievement of milestones and ultimate objectives.

FOCUS

Successful results do not happen by chance. The achievement of results depends upon maintaining focus on your goal(s) despite distractions.

- Review your priorities at the start of each workday. Give precedence to activities and tasks that support your goal by working on them first.
- Discipline yourself to have "focus time." Focus time is a period of time you set aside to concentrate all your efforts on accomplishing your goal. Minimize distractions during your "focus time" by shutting

your door, not answering emails, and letting your calls go to voice mail. Try to devote at least 1—2 hours of focus time each day to your primary goal or priority.

– Identify "time wasters" by keeping a daily log. Write down all your activities in 15-minute increments for a 1 or 2 week period. Note how much time you spend on high priority activities versus low priority tasks. Brainstorm strategies to eliminate the typical distractions and time wasters that you identified.

DEMONSTRATE ENTHUSIASM

Optimism is contagious. Share a positive attitude toward the organization and excitement about achieving goals. Words make a difference. Try to be aware of the message you are communicating to others through your comments, jokes, and expressions. Strive to consistently communicate a positive attitude and avoid making discouraging remarks about the organization, the workload, or group goals. Good or bad, others will take their cue from you.

PERSONAL RESPONSIBILITY

If you wish to challenge others to achieve results you must lead by example. While much of your work activity will probably involve coordinating and managing rather than doing the work activities that produce the results, you must commit more strongly than the people you wish to influence and must work hard if you expect others to do so. Doing some of the most difficult or unpleasant work yourself or lending a helping hand to a person or group with too much to do will also increase the commitment and effort levels of your team.Taking personal responsibility means asking yourself what you can do, and then doing it. In Personal Accountability, John Miller suggests:

— Take personal responsibility by asking questions that include "I," such as "What can I do" Initiative starts with you; do not wait for someone else to make improvements happen.

— Avoid blaming others by asking yourself questions that begin with "What" and "How" rather than "Who," "When," or "Why." For example, ask, "What can I do to increase product knowledge in my work group" instead of "Why don't they give us more product training"

— Focus on action by using words like do, achieve, and build. For example, ask yourself questions like "What can I do today to help my work group achieve its monthly production goal"

— Demonstrate your willingness to put in extra effort to achieve results. Let others see you working hard to meet or exceed goals. Offer to put in extra time to help others complete tasks related to your goals.

— Meet commitments and deadlines. If you fall behind schedule, go to work early or work late rather than asking for an extension. Others will see your commitment and are likely to follow your example.

CHALLENGE OTHERS

Challenge your team to commit to the goal and assume personal responsibility for achieving their part. Certainly, you can demand performance, and you can dictate methods and procedures to be used by all to achieve the desired result. In the long run, however, you will be more effective if you use positive and facilitative strategies such as those below.

EMPOWERMENT

Empowering others to accept responsibility and make decisions creates personal commitment to achieving results. Delegation is a key tool for encouraging others to take personal ownership for group objectives.

- Solicit input from other team members at the start of projects and throughout the initiative. Brainstorm ideas. Ask for input on decisions.
- Delegate responsibility for various aspects of the project. Ask for volunteers or assign a part of the project as a developmental opportunity for a specific team member. Delegating responsibility will help others grow in their careers and will allow you more time to focus on higher order activities.

SUPPORT

Achieving results requires more than just the will to do so. Often, people are unsure how to overcome obstacles and achieve their goals. Thus, a willingness to support, coach, and advise others in their efforts is an important component of obtaining results through others.

- Try to learn each team member's capabilities and understand their perspective of the job or project. What is working well and what can be done to improve What challenges will each individual have in trying to accomplish the group goal
- Investigate and understand the amount of work required for each task and the methods used to accomplish the task. Where in the process are obstacles likely to exist Tap the expertise of key team members to prepare for and overcome these potential setbacks.

— Strive to spend 20% of your day helping others achieve their results. Avoid detailed control of their activities, but be available to provide support on difficult issues. As problems arise, try to demonstrate how to solve the problem and discuss possible solutions rather than just providing the answers or doing the work yourself. At every opportunity, attempt to teach people how to solve the problem rather than just giving them the solution.

— Adapt your style according to individual preferences and needs. People vary in their desire for structure and guidance. Some people enjoy the freedom to accomplish goals in their own way, while other prefer the comfort of structure and guidance.

FEEDBACK AND REWARD

Reinforce hard work and accomplishment of desired results. Make a habit of rewarding top producers so that they will continue to put forth their best effort. Provide constructive feedback to those who are struggling to meet goals.

— Recognize good performance. Make a point of saying someone has done good work when they have, and make some of this praise public.

— Share the credit for achievements. Keeping the credit for yourself may bolster your personal ego in the short-term, but sharing credit will encourage results that will benefit the whole team in the long-term.

— When someone's performance falls below expectations, give him or her clear, unambiguous feedback and improvement guidance. Do this in private and with tact, but do not avoid this important responsibility.

PERSISTANCE

Ultimately, most results are achieved through a persistent, focused effort despite obstacles, fatigue, and periods of discouragement.

- Stay focused on the objective, and help others to do the same.
- Communicate with your team regularly and maintain a constant message about the importance of goal attainment.
- Recognize when interest wanes or people become discouraged. At these times, redouble your efforts to communicate, support and remove obstacles. Every difficult project will have an ebb and flow. Successful directors and their people make a habit of persisting through the low times to achieve the results they desire.

PROBLEM WITH PERFORMANCE REVIEWS

Management takes pride in producing state-of-the-art products, services, and support systems. Yet most companies are woefully lacking in the most basic, fundamental management system—the performance management process. They have archaic, worn-out programs that were designed for a different generation. They simply do not work anymore.

For most directors and employees, the performance review is like two porcupines in love—it's a pain for both parties. (However, if you want little porcupines . . . I guess that's a different book. We won't get into that here.) Many performance reviews do more harm than good. They don't help the boss-employee relationship.

They hurt it. They do not improve employee morale. They decrease it. They breed mistrust and create barriers to effective working relationships. Performance reviews have probably done more harm to employee morale than any invention since the layoff. In traditional performance review systems, directors are forced to make subjective judgements on an employee's personality, psychological makeup, and intentions. They cannot explain or defend these judgements. Neither side benefits.

Often a review is a "but-but" experience. That doesn't refer to a part of the anatomy. It means the director is the attacker and the employee is the defender. It tests the employee's stamina. The employee starts sentences with the word but: "But you didn't tell me," and "But I assumed," and "But you said," and "But this is the first I've heard of it," and "But I had no idea." Most employees give up after a few "but-but" sentences and say, "Okay, whatever you want. Let's just get this over with." They're reluctantly compliant the rest of the way. The director says, "I guess I convinced them." Then they go out and unload on other employees who sympathize with their plight, knowing their time is coming.

As students, we were given objective exams, then we were graded on our papers, had midterm tests, and took final exams. We knew how we were doing all semester long. In the work world, you're subject to the awful process of being kept in the dark for a year and then being victim of the dreaded performance review. People look forward to the review about as much as they look forward to a root canal. It's like an athlete in training for a race turning to the coach and saying, "Coach, you've got the stopwatch. How fast did I run?" The coach responds, "I'll let you know next year at your performance review." Then, the athlete says, "Coach, don't I deserve to know? How will I improve?" The coach says, "Look, if I had any problems with your performance, I'd let you know." Sound familiar? How are you going to turn out dedicated athletes that way?

Directors are uncomfortable with the performance review process. They delay it as long as they can and try to get through it as quickly as possible. They typically apologize to employees for having to subject them to the review and blame the whole mess on the human resources department.

During performance reviews, employees usually feel defenseless and taken advantage of. In another age, it was considered natural for people to feel that way. The typical employee response was, "Yes, sir. Whatever you say. Can I go now?" These days, many employees will try to give their version of what really happened, so it becomes a "but-but" review, with the employee saying, "But that's not the way things happened."

Typical Dialogue

Employees today are more astute, more aware of their rights, and have more mobility. They ask hard questions like, "What are you talking about?" Of course, some choose not to ask questions. They simply post their resume on the Internet and leave the company. A typical performance review dialogue is often an awkward, difficult experience for the director as well as the employee. Here's a typical exchange:

Director: I rate you "below average" in versatility [or any of the other murky behaviour characteristics found on check-off-the-box forms].

Employee: I don't understand. Below average in relation to whom or what? How have you measured the versatility of everyone else? What is versatility, anyhow? We have gone an entire year and this is the first time you have used that word. If it's so important, why haven't you mentioned it until today?

Director: I'm not sure what they mean by it. It's here on the form and I have to check it off. I'm not sure what any of these things mean. I'm sorry. I've been so busy. Let's just get this over with. So, I rate you average in citizenship. Your teamwork needs improvement. Pretty good in your work habits . . .

Employee: Look. I can appreciate the fact that you have problems, but why should I be penalized for that? If you had any issues with my performance, why didn't you tell me? Why wait until now when it's too late to do anything about it?

Director: I'm sorry. It won't happen again. I should have talked to you about it before.

Employee: That's what you told me last year. And the year before that. And the year before that.

Clearly, the deck is stacked against the director with the old-fashioned performance review. Employees may not actually say the words the employee said in the example. They think them, though. Worse still, many performance reviews are late. My daughter, Lori, has a birthday on March 5. A late performance review is like saying "Happy Birthday" to her on September 5. It sort of loses its punch, doesn't it? I'd compound the oversight if I told her how busy I was and how I didn't have time for her over the last six months. She'd say, "If you don't have time for me, Dad, don't expect me to have time for you."

How to Do It Right?

Can this mess be turned into something useful? Yes! It begins with following a logical sequence using up-to-date assumptions about employees. It puts the *performance* back in performance review. It recognizes that employees are adults, not children. They are citizens, voters, and taxpayers. They deserve to be treated as responsible, intelligent, important members of the organization. If a director expects responsible, adult behaviour from an employee, the director must treat the employee in a responsible, adult manner. A review should be a discussion between two people that reviews information. Nothing new should be introduced. Nothing in it should be a surprise. Furthermore, the performance management process should be year-round. There's no way a productive discussion can be held once a year on someone's performance.

Making the process useful takes an understanding of the real purpose of performance reviews. It's to improve employee performance. Employees crave recognition and positive reinforcement. They want to feel that their work is recognized and appreciated. Imagine how useful this process would be if an employee went away feeling that the review was a complete, accurate description of actual contributions over the past year. Written praise for past achievements and recognition of special accomplishments are strong motivators for the employee. Instead, as we all know, employees too often say, "The director doesn't even know what we do." That doesn't stop their directors from giving them their performance reviews, though.

Better Dialogue

Directors should do the performance review with and not for the employee. Even if a director had to use a system that talks about behaviour characteristics, the dialogue should be something like this:

Director: The next category is initiative. How would that apply to your job?

Employee: I guess that would mean doing things on my own and not waiting to be asked.

Director: How do you think you've done on that?

Employee: Okay, I guess. I probably could have done more.

Director: Such as?

Employee: Well, we've talked about . . .

Three Essential Steps

A good performance management process is made up of three essential steps:

1. *Goal-Setting.* The director and employee negotiate what has to be accomplished during the performance review period. Goals must be SMART—specific, measurable, achievable, results-oriented, and time-bounded. If annual goals are not practical, then monthly or even weekly goals should be set. The director and employee should meet for renegotiation as often as necessary. As the employee, knowing what you're supposed to do puts you at a powerful advantage over most people. It used to be that jobs were clearly defined and very straightforward. Accountants, for example, kept the books. They put the debits on the left and the credits on the right. Today, computers do the routine work. We expect our professionals to analyze, influence, persuade, and inform. They have to be clever enough to unravel the mystery of how their success will be measured. Once you know how your performance will be evaluated, you then can intelligently structure your day. So many people, unfortunately, don't know what's important in their job and they can't structure their day. The day structures them. They drift from one thing to another. They go with the flow. And the "you know what" flows downhill.
2. *Progress Reviews.* The director and employee periodically discuss job performance. The employee

brings in action plans for approval, recommends corrective action for problem resolution, and offers ideas for development actions. If the director has a problem with any area of the employee's performance, this is the time for bringing it up. It should not be saved up for the annual performance review. This way, the director is helping the employee to remedy the problem before it's documented and viewed by the employee as unfair punishment. If all is going well, this is an ideal time for the director to give sincere, specific, positive reinforcement. Without praise, employees assume that the director is only going to pay attention to them when there are problems. That often gives rise to more problems. This exchange is *not* a progress review:

Director: How's it going?

Employee: Good.

Director: Any problems

Employee: Nothing I can't handle.

Director: So, I can count on you to get your goals accomplished?

Employee: I'll do the best I can.

Director: Great. Glad we had this little talk.

This exchange is worth nothing. It's a waste of time. The director who has vague, pointless discussions like that is going to get some nasty surprises in the end.

3. *Performance Reviews.* No new information is introduced at the annual performance review. The director and employee should document what has been discussed previously in progress reviews. There should be no forced distribution of performance ratings. This is a bad tradition that

serves no purpose. Imagine if I had to rate my four children and the ratings had to fall into a normal distribution, so I was forced to call one of them above average, two of them average, and one of them below average. It would serve no useful purpose. They're *all* wonderful! Why would I want to destroy my relationship with them with such foolishness? I'd have to say the kind of hogwash that many directors do: "I'm sorry, but the system requires me to call one of you below average. You're really wonderful, but it's your turn this time. Everyone else has had to take a hit. It's your turn."

Goal Setting

Many so-called goals are not worth the paper they're printed on. Something like "Learn and grow" or "Improve your relationships with the field organization" or "Continue to work on special projects" doesn't mean anything. All goals should be stated in specific terms that identify precisely what, when, and to what extent something must be done. All goals should be output-oriented (i.e., focused on results) and typically fall into one of three categories:

1. *Routine/Maintenance Goals.* Activities that are repetitive, ongoing, and currently functioning at acceptable levels. These goals do not change present status but seek to maintain it.
2. *Improvement/Problem-Solving Goals.* A problem situation exists that requires a change from X to Y.
3. *Innovation/Creative Goals.* New ideas, new projects, or changes in technology are needed to create something that hasn't existed before.

Be sure not to fall into the trap of discussing salary increases at performance review time. Raises are based on a variety of factors with performance being only one of them—and often not the most important determinant. The other factors are usually job grade, performance of others in the job category, and particular corporate guidelines for the review period. Discussing salary diverts attention from the real issue during the performance review process, which is improving performance. So have separate meetings for the performance review and salary discussion.

Directors who say they don't have time for goal-setting, progress reviews, and performance reviews are saying they don't understand why their job exists. It's like Rembrandt saying he doesn't have time to paint, Einstein saying he's too busy to work with numbers, or Jonas Salk saying he'll invent vaccines someday if he gets around to it. Helping employees succeed is not something directors do only if they have time available after they get their job done. It *is* their job. Anything else is secondary.

Two-Way Communication

During a goal-setting, progress review, or performance review session, the employee should do most of the talking. The directors should ask questions and do a lot of listening. Outstanding directors stress collaborative goals. They are clear about the specific results they want to achieve. They don't speak in terms such as "Do your best" or "See what you can do." They take complex projects and break them down into achievable steps. They actively involve others in planning, giving them as much discretion as possible to make their own decisions. Overall, this isn't just the best way to deal with your employees, it's becoming the only way as employees become smarter and more demanding.

It would be a really good idea if you made giving feedback a two-way process. People appreciate relationships that are give-and-take. A marriage that is only one way—with one giver and one taker—is usually an unhappy one. If you're going to give the employee feedback, as you certainly should, it only seems reasonable that the employee give you some feedback. The wrong way to do this is to ask leading questions. For instance, you won't learn much if you say, "I'm a terrific director, aren't I?" or "You don't have any problems with me, do you?" Instead, have various ways to get feedback in individual as well as group settings.

Today's employees increasingly aren't accepting a passive role in a process that helps determine their career success. To generate accurate and meaningful reviews of past performance, directors need the perspective of the employee. A self-appraisal should always be part of the performance review process. It requires employees to actively participate in their own evaluations. The director first solicits input from the employee in order to help generate an accurate review. The employee, in turn, gains a better understanding of, and commitment to, the whole review process.

Rather than being pitted against one another in a power struggle, the director and employee should cooperate to identify the employee's accomplishments. As part of this process, areas needing improvement should be discussed in a constructive manner that emphasizes how results can be better achieved in the future. If the director focuses on what someone did wrong, it's typically seen as blaming. If the director focuses on what someone can do better in the future, it's typically seen as a development discussion and things will go much smoother. Input from other sources should be gathered to increase the accuracy of the review. Objective measures that reflect the subordinate's performance from the perspective of external or internal customers can be particularly valuable.

The director and employee can choose any appropriate collaborative method to complete the review form. After that, there are several possibilities:

— The employee completes a self-appraisal and the director then completes a draft of the review form, and they negotiate any differences between the two versions.

— The director and employee jointly complete the review form together.

— The employee completes a self-appraisal and it is edited by the director prior to being written in final form.

— The director completes the review form and the employee self-appraisal is attached to it, with both documents becoming a part of the employee's file.

How to Give a Merit Increase?

There's often an uneasy relationship between the human resources department and the directors in an organization. From the HR standpoint, directors don't bother to learn the policies and procedures of the organization. From the directors' standpoint, human resources doesn't explain what those policies and procedures are, or the reasons for them. HR just assumes that directors are supposed to know what they are and how to administer them. It's one of those arguments where both sides are right. At salary increase time, many directors aren't sure of what to say to their employees, so they say nothing.

Assuming you have job grades and ranges in your organization, it's all about midpoint control. If you don't know if you have job grades and ranges, you should find out. A range consists of a minimum, midpoint, and maximum for each grade level. The ranges are usually reviewed once a year in a company, although not necessarily changed. The real value of a job is the midpoint. Individual performance is measured against the midpoint with the "fully competent employee" expected to be paid about that amount.

If performance is less than what you'd expect of an employee in that position—for example, because someone is learning the job—pay should be in the lower half of the range. The upper part of the range is reserved for those whose performance is above what you'd expect of an employee in that position. Therefore, employee salaries grow through the range only when performance constantly improves. Salaries level off when performance levels off. When that happens, an employee may get no increase or simply a raise consistent with the amount that the salary range moves.

Table 1 is a five-factor performance rating system. It shows why someone who, for example, never moves past "Fully meets requirements" will never move past the midpoint of the range. Someone who gets a zero percent increase would either have to improve his performance or get a promotion to a higher grade level in order to be eligible for a salary increase the next time around.

Table 1. Five-factor performance review system.

Sample Salary Guidelines				
Far Exceeds	8–10%	6–8%	4–6%	2–4%
Usually Exceeds	6–8%	4–6%	2–4%	0–2%
Fully Meets	4–6%	2–4%	0–2%	0%
Usually Meets	2–4%	0–2%	0%	0%
Below Requirements	0-2%	0%	0%	0%
	1st Quartile	2nd Quartile	3rd Quartile	4th Quartile

This commonly used salary matrix considers job performance and position in the salary range. When talking to your employees, show them the matrix and then review job performance by referring to previous performance review discussions and pointing out position in the range.

Remember, the worst kind of salary discussion is when the director doesn't take the time to discuss compenzation practices or doesn't have the knowledge to do it. Just saying, "You're getting a 5 per cent increase. That's all there is to it," is not a businesslike, professional statement. The complete requirements for an effective merit increase discussion are as follows:

- *Be precise.* Explain your company's salary policy clearly and concisely. Make sure you let employees know their present salary grade and the salary range. Let the employee know the amount and effective date of the increase.
- *Review the performance data upon which the salary decision was made.* If employees have concerns over the salary decision, don't argue with them. Respond openly and with empathy. Provide as much objective data as you can about the issues raised by each employee. The only "off limits" area of discussion should be the salary of other employees.
- *Make sure employees understand that the increase corresponds to their overall performance rating.* For example, a rating of "Usually exceeds requirements" for a person in the second quartile would normally result in an increase within the guidelines for that category. Try to carefully explain the rationale behind the amount of the increase.
- *Do not negotiate salary.* If you've done a good job of explaining the salary policy and have fairly

evaluated the employee's performance, there's no need for you to feel defensive or apologetic. Don't blame "them," or "the system," or "the boss." Take ownership of the salary decision.

If the employee is unhappy with the increase, you should discuss how the person can increase her contributions to the organization, which could increase the likelihood of a larger increase in the future. Be careful not to make any promises you won't be able to keep. Remember the unknowns you're dealing with. The next performance review rating will be affected by the performance of others in the department and the amount of the merit budget will be affected by the salary plans of other companies as well as the financial performance of your own company. Be careful. You don't want irate people telling you later, "You promised me . . . ."

If you feel someone is being unfairly compensated, discuss this with your director and human resources. Do this long before salary increase time. I can guarantee if you march down to human resources because your people have complained that their annual salary increases were inadequate, you'll get a defensive reaction from human resources. Instead, begin to work the issue months in advance.

Human resources, hopefully, conducts an annual salary survey and can tell you if the person is competitively paid based on what others make both inside and outside your company. If an equity adjustment in base salary isn't appropriate, there might be other aspects of total compenzation that can be examined—for example, a onetime bonus, stock options, or an increased salary incentive program. If HR indicates the person is fairly paid, you then have to buckle up and tell the person that research indicates his compenzation is at an appropriate level. That's usually called "taking ownership," and that's what directors have to do.

Development Planning

Development planning is often dreaded by employees. Like the performance review, this process too often is a chance for a director to "beat up" on an employee. People are told, "In order to be more well rounded you need to do . . . ." Frankly, the only people who need to be well rounded are cartoon characters. We tend to want to produce people who are "jacks of all trades and masters of none." People become successful not because they are well rounded or have an absence of weaknesses. They become successful because they have an expertise in something. That something should be based on what they love doing and have a passion for, and it must meet the needs of the organization. For too many directors, the only consideration is the needs of the organization. A more useful development plan is one where the director asks questions rather than dictates development activities. Simple, straightforward questions such as:

- What do you want to become better at, either to improve current performance or prepare for greater responsibility?
- What kinds of activities would help you do that?

If employees aren't sure of what they want to do, that's fine. There should be a plan to help determine that. They could do information interviewing with members of management or other employees. They could shadow people on the job. They could work on a developmental assignment in a different department. They may learn that they like or don't like something. Either way, that's good to know.

Be careful not to talk to people about things they don't want to and don't have to do. For example, an individual development plan sounds like a good idea. But the way it's often implemented is a turn-off for many people. The director may use it like a performance review—as a weapon to discuss someone's "weaknesses." Often, people are given lists of things they need to "do better" whether they want to or not. Instead, I'd recommend building on someone's strengths and interests. Typically the stronger people are in their area of specialty, the weaker they are in other things. In other words, someone who is a world-class pianist probably hasn't taken the time to learn to drive, to go out on dates, or to develop a taste for fine wines. Build on people's strengths. Don't dwell on their weaknesses. Talk to the world-class pianist about what interests him—playing the piano— and not about things he doesn't care about.

Here's how ridiculous many development discussions are. Let's say you were having one with Bill Gates. Imagine if it went like this:"Hi, Bill. It's time for our annual development discussion. You've concentrated on being a CEO and now you're going to be working full time on running your charitable organization. That's all well and good, but it's my job to point out the things you don't do well. So, I've written up a few of them. You don't know how to do needlepoint, so I've arranged for a class on it for you. Furthermore, you don't speak Swahili, so I suggest you take an online course to learn that language. I've also seen, in examining your records, that you aren't very good at curling. So, I'm going to ask you to join our company curling team. Okay, Bill. That's it for this time around. See you next year."

Maybe, unlike most employees, Bill dares to question management. He says, "But I'm not interested in any of those things. I don't want to do them." You'd say, "Look, Bill. I know what's best for you. I *strongly* suggest you follow my suggestions. You don't want to be accused of having a bad attitude, do you?" So, Bill leaves your office feeling defeated and discouraged. You check off the box that you've had another development discussion.

❖❖❖

8

MANAGING ORGANIZATIONAL CHANGE

Managing organizational change will be more successful if you apply these simple principles. Achieving personal change will be more successful too if you use the same approach where relevant. Change management entails thoughtful planning and sensitive implementation, and above all, consultation with, and involvement of, the people affected by the changes. If you force change on people normally problems arise.

Change must be realistic, achievable and measurable. These aspects are especially relevant to managing personal change. Before starting organizational change, ask yourself: What do we want to achieve with this change, why, and how will we know that the change has been achieved? Who is affected by this change, and how will they react to it? How much of this change can we achieve ourselves, and what parts of the change do we need help with? These aspects also relate strongly to the management of personal as well as organizational change.

Do not 'sell' change to people as a way of accelerating 'agreement' and implementation. 'Selling' change to people is not a sustainable strategy for success, unless your aim is to be bitten on the bum at some time in the future when you least expect it. When people listen to a management high-up 'selling' them a change, decent diligent folk will generally smile and appear to accede, but quietly to themselves, they're thinking, "No bloody chance mate, if you think I'm standing for that load of old bollocks you've another think coming..."

The employee does not have a responsibility to manage change—the employee's responsibility is no other than to do their best, which is different for every person and depends on a wide variety of factors (health, maturity, stability, experience, personality, motivation, etc.). Responsibility for managing change is with management and executives of the organization—they must manage the change in a way that employees can cope with it. The director has a responsibility to facilitate and enable change, and all that is implied within that statement, especially to understand the situation from an objective standpoint (to 'step back', and be non-judgemental), and then to help people understand reasons, aims, and ways of responding positively according to employees' own situations and capabilities. Increasingly the director 's role is to interpret, communicate and enable—not to instruct and impose, which nobody really responds to well.

CHANGE MUST INVOLVE THE PEOPLE

Be wary of expressions like 'mindset change', and 'changing people's mindsets' or 'changing attitudes', because this language often indicates a tendency towards imposed or enforced change, and it implies strongly that the organization believes that its people currently have the 'wrong' mindset, which is never, ever, the case. If people are not approaching their tasks or the organization effectively, then the organization has the wrong mindset, not the people. Change such as new structures, policies, targets, acquisitions, disposals, relocations, etc., all create new systems and environments, which need to be explained to people as early as possible, so that people's involvement in validating and refining the changes themselves can be obtained.

Whenever an organization imposes new things on people there will be difficulties. Participation, involvement and open, early, full communication are the important factors.

Workshops are very useful processes to develop collective understanding, approaches, policies, methods, systems, ideas, etc. See the section on workshops on the website.

Staff surveys are a helpful way to repair damage and mistrust among staff—provided you allow allow people to complete them anonymously, and provided you publish and act on the findings.

Management training, empathy and facilitative capability are priority areas—managers are crucial to the change process—they must enable and facilitate, not merely convey and implement policy from above, which does not work.

You cannot impose change—people and teams need to be empowered to find their own solutions and responses, with facilitation and support from managers, and tolerance and compassion from the leaders and executives. Management and leadership style and behaviour are more important than clever process and policy. Employees need to be able to trust the organization.

The leader must agree and work with these ideas, or change is likely to be very painful, and the best people will be lost in the process.

CHANGE MANAGEMENT PRINCIPLES

Here are some modern principles for organizational change management and effective employee training and development. These principles are for forward-thinking emotionally-mature organizations, who value integrity above results, and people above profit.

- At all times involve and agree support from people within system (system = environment, processes, culture, relationships, behaviours, etc., whether personal or organizational).
- Understand where you/the organization is at the moment.
- Understand where you want to be, when, why, and what the measures will be for having got there.
- Plan development towards above No.3 in appropriate achievable measurable stages.
- Communicate, involve, enable and facilitate involvement from people, as early and openly and as fully as is possible.

KOTTER'S 'EIGHT STEPS TO SUCCESSFUL CHANGE'

American John P Kotter is a Harvard Business School professor and leading thinker and author on organizational change management. Kotter's highly regarded books 'Leading Change' and the follow-up 'The Heart Of Change' describe a helpful model for understanding and managing change. Each stage acknowledges a key principle identified by Kotter relating to people's response and approach to change, in which people see, feel and then change.

Kotter's eight step change model can be summarised as:

- *Increase urgency*—inspire people to move, make objectives real and relevant.

- *Build the guiding team*—get the right people in place with the right emotional commitment, and the right mix of skills and levels.
- *Get the vision right*—get the team to establish a simple vision and strategy, focus on emotional and creative aspects necessary to drive service and efficiency.
- *Communicate for buy-in*—Involve as many people as possible, communicate the essentials, simply, and to appeal and respond to people's needs. De-clutter communications—make technology work for you rather than against.
- *Empower action*—Remove obstacles, enable constructive feedback and lots of support from leaders—reward and recognise progress and achievements.
- *Create short-term wins*—Set aims that are easy to achieve—in bite-size chunks. Manageable numbers of initiatives. Finish current stages before starting new ones.
- *Don't let up*—Foster and encourage determination and persistence—ongoing change—encourage ongoing progress reporting—highlight achieved and future milestones.
- *Make change stick*—Reinforce the value of successful change via recruitment, promotion, new change leaders. Weave change into culture.

STAGES OF TRANSITION THROUGH CHANGE

Conventional wisdom is that people resist change. That's not quite true. People resist being changed. We don't like to be forced to do things without an explanation. That's the way it happens too often at work. Information is essential to employees during change. They need to know exactly what needs to be done, how it needs to be done, and why it needs to be done. Many people feel uncertain and insecure during times of change. Most directors don't do a good job of providing information when things are in a normal state, let alone during times of significant change.

People transition through the change process in a predictable way. Almost everybody in almost every situation goes through the same basic stages. Some theorists have put forth a five-stage system; some talk about six stages, some seven. The U-shaped arrow shown in Figure 1 represents energy.

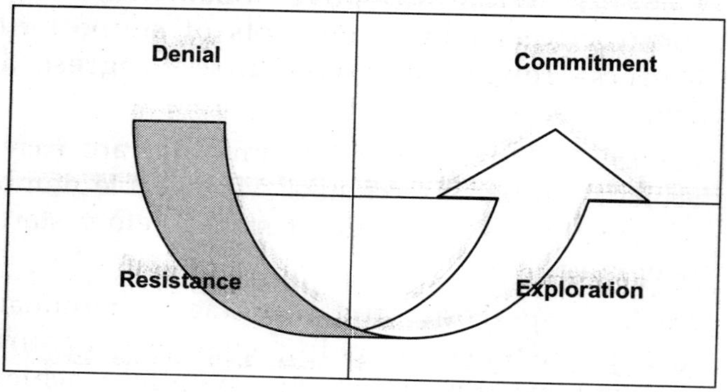

Figure 1. Stages of the change process

It can take days, weeks, months, or years to go all the way from the first stage to the final stage. Furthermore, there's no guarantee that someone will go all the way from the first to the final stage. It's very possible that someone could get stuck in a stage and stay there. It's unlikely that someone can skip stages. It's very rare that someone fails to go through these stages in the exact order presented. Change is like a traumatic event. It's easy to say "Just get over it!" but some people can't. It can stay with them a lifetime. The director's job is not to prevent change. It's to get people to progress through the stages and get to the final one—commitment—as soon as possible. The stages are:

1. *Denial.* The immediate impact of the change is usually numbness. Someone doesn't know what to think. The safest thing to do, then, is to take a "wait and see" approach. "We'll cross that bridge when we come to it," or "You don't really believe that stuff, do you?" are common responses to major changes. A woman whose husband dies after fifty years of marriage might continue to wash his clothes, for example, and hang them in the closet. She's confused and really can't handle the change. "I just wish everyone would stop telling me what to do, she says, "I'll deal with this when I'm ready."
2. *Resistance.* There are two types of resistance—active and passive. Active resistance is when someone openly rebels against the change. It's easier for a director to deal with active resistance because people come and tell you what they think. Passive resistance is much more common. It's when someone pays you lip service but withdraws their energy and enthusiasm. They might sabotage something by "forgetting" about it or "not having enough time" to do it. The newly widowed woman might "forget" about the appointment with the lawyer to discuss the execution of her husband's will. Or she "agrees" to fill out the insurance claim form but conveniently "loses" it. The focus during this stage is inward—people feeling sorry for themselves.
3. *Exploration.* Most healthy people after a suitable period of time will progress to the exploration stage, which involves thinking about and planning for the future. All of a sudden, the widow takes her

husband's clothes from the closet and is ready to donate them to charity. One day she begins to talk about what she's going to do with the insurance money. Relatives might say, "We've been telling you this for months. It's about time." The truth is, she's ready now. She wasn't before. Now she has the mental and physical energy to look to the future.

4. *Commitment.* It's conceivable, but remember, not a given, that someone can go to the final stage. This is when they've embraced the change, wrestled with it, examined possibilities, and now they're ready to move on. It's conceivable that they can be just as energetic and enthusiastic as they were before. In a company that has had a layoff, for instance, it may be a year or more before people get to this stage. You know that the widow in the example has gotten to the final stage when she's doing things she wasn't doing before—maybe buying new clothes, or joining a health club, or wanting to travel with friends.

"Supporting" Employee Movement Through the Stages

When information is poor, employees are more likely to feel anxious and insecure. They'll have trouble progressing through the stages. People who hear nothing usually fear the worst. What they dream up in the way of rumours is usually significantly worse than the truth of the situation. What can directors do to help? It can be summarized with the acronym Supporting:

— Seeing other people's point of view

— Unrestricted access to information

— Positive thinking and optimism

— Presence and proximity

- Openness to the effects of the change
- Rumours and gossip openly discussed
- Thanking people for their cooperation and flexibility
- Involvement
- No change in values
- Guidance

When I talk about the importance of "presence and proximity," it is because many directors make the mistake of disappearing during times of change or spend their days huddled with other directors behind closed doors. Involvement means that the more you share information and use people's ideas, the better they'll adapt to the change. You can also help employees by showing "no change in values," which means you should believe in the same things and stand for the same things in good times or bad. Finally, it's perfectly okay for you to say things like, "Here's what I think, " or "Here's my take on things," or "Here's the way I look at it." Many directors are afraid to give any guidance for fear that they'll be wrong. Sharing your personal opinion is always appropriate, even if you turn out to be wrong. People will still appreciate it.

When directors introduce change to the work group, they need to be thoroughly prepared with detailed background information. Time invested in gathering information will save considerable time and anguish in the future. If your director doesn't know the reasons for the change and the impact it will have in your work group, find out who does. Get the information you need from that person. It is much easier and more efficient to take an approach that will prevent resistance before a change takes place rather than having to deal with resistance that has been built up after the change.

Explain completely how the change will affect your employees because this information will be their primary area of concern. The atmosphere of openness you create by asking for, and accepting, their reactions will help make them more receptive to the change. In fact, if the initial reaction is positive, ask them if they see any negative aspects of the change. Conversely, if the initial reaction is negative, ask for positive aspects. Do not avoid discussion of the unfavourable effects. The employees will experience them sooner or later, and if the employees bring these unfavourable effects to your attention later, they are more likely to voice them in anger as complaints.

By dealing with employee concerns openly, you will do much to alleviate their anxieties and reduce the threat of the change. Be sure to involve them as much as possible in all aspects of the change. Ask for employee ideas and use them, if at all possible. If a change is nonnegotiable, let your people know that. Tell them, "We need to implement this new policy and I need your ideas on how to make it work."

You may find certain employees will just not agree with the need for change. If this occurs, your task is not to argue or become defensive, but to accept the fact there may be an honest difference of opinion. Even though not everyone agrees with the change, don't be afraid to ask for a commitment to making the change successful. If you've done a good job in earning respect and credibility, you will likely have the loyalty of your employees. This, then, is a time when it may be appropriate for you to say things such as, "Could you do me a favour?" and "I'd appreciate your doing this for me."

HANDLING PERFORMANCE PROBLEMS

A lot of people equate discipline with punishing or

hurting someone. They equate it with the discipline they received as a child—getting yelled at and maybe spanked. A more appropriate, adult-like way to look at discipline is holding people accountable for what they agree they're going to do. It's as simple as that. Once they commit to do something, they should be expected to do it. For instance, if you were the admiral in charge of an aircraft carrier group cruising in the Persian Gulf, you'd have someone assigned to a midnight watch. You would expect that person to actually show up. If he didn't, you'd put that person in the brig and brought up on serious charges. There are people "not showing up" in organizations every day. What happens to them? Nothing! Absolutely nothing! The people in a department say, "Why doesn't management do something about it?" The assumption is: "Because management doesn't really care." The director usually gives a feeble excuse such as, "I don't want to upset 8anyone," or "I'm afraid that I'd make matters worse."

Dealing with Causes, Not Symptoms

If directors would only ask "Why?" more than they do, life would be better for everyone. That way you'd be dealing with causes and not symptoms. I can't tell you how many directors, for instance, came into my office and said something like, "I want to fire this person who has a terrible absentee problem." Most of the time, by the way, in a situation like that, the employee would admit skipping work "because I can't stand my director and I need a mental health day from time to time." Dig down and find out why people do what they do and why they feel the way they do. A woman in labour has a bad attitude. When someone has a bad attitude, isn't motivated, makes too many errors, or whatever the problem might be, it would help to find out what's causing the problem. Then, have them agree to a solution and hold them accountable for those actions. After getting the person to admit that a problem does indeed exist, then:

- As a first choice, have them come up with the possible solutions to the problem. People are much more likely to make their own ideas work.
- If they can't come up with possible solutions, give them a little time. Say, "Why don't you think about it overnight and we'll meet first thing tomorrow."
- If they still can't or won't give you solutions, then give them a list of possibilities and ask them which are the most practical.
- If they can't or won't choose anything from the list you've offered, give them a little time to "think about it overnight," then meet with them again the next day.
- As an absolute last resort, tell them what they should do. This is when your back is against the wall. Recognize it will be "your idea" and not "their idea," so it's likely they won't have much commitment.

Whatever ideas you and the person agree upon, be sure to write them down. The employee may become anxious and say, "Are you writing me up?" I've learned the best thing to say at that point is, "No, I'm writing it down. That way neither one of us will forget what we've agreed to." The connotation of "writing someone up" is that you're going to get rid of them and just need some documentation. The connotation of "writing it down" should be to approach things in a businesslike way, so it's an agreement that can be referred to later.

Imagine going to a doctor and saying, "Can you give me something for my headache?" An experienced doctor uses the headache as a symptom of a problem. If you've got a brain tumour, that's the real cause. Cure the brain tumour and the headache goes away. Almost all employee performance problems are symptoms. You've got to find the cause and then take corrective action.

Address performance problems early. It's much easier to say to someone, "I noticed something that I want to point out to you. It's not a big deal and will be easy for you to correct. I just want to mention it before it becomes a problem." Most people wouldn't react badly to that kind of comment. Contrast that with the director who says, "I've had it with you. You've been a poor performer for the last twenty-three years and I'm sick of it."

Get employee agreement that they have to make a change in their behaviour. You can ask them to send you an e-mail, to confirm that they will make the change. On something significant, remember, you'll want to know exactly *how* they're going to do it.

Then schedule a follow-up date to review progress. Without a follow-up date, people are likely to assume that you weren't serious about the matter in the first place. If things go well and there's improvement, it gives you an opportunity to praise and thank employees for their efforts. If things don't go well, you once again get their commitment and speak in stronger terms about the need for the change. However, don't threaten people. Most of the time, they'll react very negatively. Even if you have a written action plan stating that "failure to meet the terms of this agreement will result in further disciplinary action, up to and including termination," you're still on the employee's side. You should tell everyone, "I certainly don't want disciplinary action to happen. I have every confidence that you'll be able to fulfil the terms of our agreement. I'll do everything possible to help you." Don't ever give employees the feeling that you're "out to get them."

Make sure you let employees know *why* something is a problem. For example, if they're continually late, don't just say, "It's against our policy" to be late. Instead, say, "You've missed the first part of our product strategy meeting three times in the last three weeks. I need your input in those meetings. You're in direct contact with our field people and you're expected to present their viewpoint at these meetings." If people understand the reason why you need them to change their behaviour, they're much more likely to do it. Everyone everywhere belongs to Generation "Why." A key management responsibility is not just to let them know you want something, but to explain *why* you want it, too.

Giving Feedback

When you give feedback, make sure it's timely. Don't save it up. If you said to someone, "That was a good meeting you ran last February," the person would probably say, "What meeting?" You then reply, "I don't really remember. I just have a note here to mention it to you. I've been carrying the note around for about ten months." If you're going to compliment someone about a meeting, do it right away. Even positive feedback will backfire if it's not timely. Saying, "Nice job on that project," doesn't mean much if it's six years later.

Make sure your feedback is about behaviour that can be changed. Frustration is increased when you remind people of shortcomings over which they have no control. It's like saying, "I think you're too short. Why don't you grow?" Also be sure to objectively describe observed behaviour and results rather than evaluate the individual. If you avoid evaluation, you reduce the likelihood of a defensive reaction.

Don't give employees negative feedback when you're angry with them. You'll say things you don't mean and you'll say things you're sorry for afterward. Be professional, calm, and objective. Talk facts and don't exaggerate. Avoid words like "Always" or "Never" because they invite the other person to bring up the exceptions to prove you wrong. Instead, use more conservative phrases like "You have a tendency" or "A number of times" or "Often." That way it will be very difficult for them to bring up the exceptions to prove you wrong.

Don't try to make people into something they're not. It's like they're chess pieces. They're all different and they all have certain abilities. Don't try to make a knight into a rook. Don't try to make a pawn into a bishop. Respect employees for what they are. It is management's job to win the chess game, given the pieces it has. Learn to use the pieces better.

The best way to think of yourself is as a teacher. The employee is your disciple. The word disciple actually means learner. So, when you're applying discipline, you're operating in a teaching mode. Let employees know in no uncertain terms what they can do better and teach them how to do it better or have someone else teach them. Criticizing or punishing them is not teaching them anything, other than to dislike and maybe avoid the person doing the criticizing or punishing. It's good that you want to give someone some feedback, but don't say, "You're not a team player. I want you to work on that." They'll have no idea what you want them to do. A teacher wouldn't simply say to a student, "I want you to learn about differential equations." It's your job to teach them. The best directors are always the best teachers.

The Frankenstein Syndrome

There's a tale of Gothic horror that strikes fear in the hearts and minds of people everywhere. No, it isn't Mary Shelley's *Frankenstein.* It's the story of the director-employee relationship that's created in far too many instances in today's workplace. Although published in 1818, *Frankenstein* is disturbingly similar to what often happens in modern organizational life. The story can help directors understand how they can take good, decent people and turn them into cynical, bitter employees. These employees become shells of the enthusiastic, positive people they were when they joined the company. It leads to the "Frankenstein syndrome," where directors create their own monsters. Just like in the book, it's the poor monster who gets the blame. But who created the monster? Isn't Dr. Frankenstein at least partly at fault?

Why does it happen? In interviews, directors often describe idyllic job situations that bear little relationship to reality. They don't describe the way things are. They describe the way they *wish* things were. The director says, "This company recognizes people for their contributions and provides unlimited growth opportunity. In addition, encourage innovation, and provide as much responsibility as people can handle." Applicants leave with stars in their eyes, telling the folks back home what a great boss and great company they are joining. The directors are delighted to have the "old" or malcontent employee leave the job and welcome the bright, enthusiastic, and positive newcomer.

So, a new employee is hired. The director, however, is unavailable during much of the employee's first day of work (or any day thereafter). The new hire soon realizes that the job is mundane, repetitive, and lacking in any real responsibility. The employee becomes disillusioned and frustrated. The director asks for ideas but never does anything with them. She says, "My door is always open," but doesn't listen to what the employee says. She offers to investigate the situation and get back to the employee, but never does.

In addition, the director withholds information, telling the employee that certain situations are management confidential and that employees do not have a need to know. If the employee tries to approach the director, the answer is always, "Now is not a good time. Wait for things to settle down." Ideas and suggestions are met with responses such as, "That's not the way we do things around here."

There are numerous other frustrating incidents, such as the director saying that a project has to be completed "first thing tomorrow morning."

The employee works through most of the night to get it done. Then, it sits on the director's desk untouched for weeks. The employee longs for the management style that the director spoke of during the interview but never has practiced. It's just as the monster in Frankenstein said: "Everywhere I see bliss, from which I alone am irrevocably excluded. I was benevolent and good; misery made me a fiend."

The director is offended and becomes defensive, accusing the employee of having the infamous bad attitude. There's a power struggle between the director and the monster—employee. After being accused of having a bad attitude by the director, the employee, of course, does indeed develop a really bad attitude, just as the monster did: "I will work at your destruction, nor finish until I desolate your heart, so that you shall curse the hour of your birth."

The employee manages to tough it out for a year, but the first performance review is a disaster. The director discusses attitude, personality, and intentions. The employee doesn't understand why these topics are being brought up and wants to know when the director will begin discussing job performance. The employee complains of not being treated as a professional. The director feels she has hired the wrong person. The employee feels the director is out to get him. The director goes to human resources and, as has happened many times before, makes remarks about the ungrateful, disrespectful employee. Dr. Frankenstein sums it up, expressing the desire "to wreak a great and signal revenge on his cursed head."

The HR director thinks, "Just another personality conflict. A transfer is out of the question because no one will accept an employee with a bad attitude. Our directors have more than enough people like that already."

This brings the matter full circle. The employee goes on job interviews, citing lack of recognition, growth, appreciation, or responsibility as his reasons for wanting to change jobs. He describes the current job in words similar to Frankenstein's monster: "a hell of intense tortures, such as no language can describe." His new boss promises what the employee is looking for and the employee is impressed. He goes home saying, "What a great company and great boss I'm joining."

The old director goes through the motions and says she is sorry to see the employee leave and wishes him well. She breathes a sigh of relief, though, because there will not be any more problems with this employee.

Just as Dr. Frankenstein lamented: "I lived in daily fear, lest the monster whom I had created should perpetrate some new wickedness." Thus, the story ends with the director again trying to locate the best person to fill the job and describing an idyllic job situation. . . . The parallel between the story of Frankenstein and the director is certainly a cause for concern. In the world of management, you often get what you have created.

Outstanding directors mold and nurture the people they hire—their "creations"—the same way they would nurture a child. Rather than focusing on weaknesses, they build on people's strengths. The best directors are gifted in being able to structure jobs, projects, and organizations so that talents and strengths are fully utilized and the impact of weaknesses is minimal. They bring out the best in people.

Think of the kind of support a leader gives people in any field of human endeavour. The leader says, "I know you can do it," while the follower says, "I'm not good enough. I can't do it." The persistence of the leader can be convincing. All of the successful people I know can point to someone who believed in them. They say, "There was someone who wouldn't let me quit. They were there to pick me up when I fell down. Without them, I wouldn't have made it." I don't know of a single exception. Every successful person has had someone like that in his life.

You can be that person! What an exciting opportunity for you. Someday, someone can say about you, "I owe it all to you. You said that you knew I could do it. You said I was good enough. You were there to pick me up when I fell down. Thank you." As a director, you can make that kind of difference in someone's life. Maybe even a lot of someones.

❖❖❖

9

DEVELOPING LEADERSHIP QUALITIES

What is leadership? It is a process by which one person influences the thoughts, attitudes, and behaviours of others. Leaders set a direction for the rest of us; they help us see what lies ahead; they help us visualize what we might achieve; they encourage us and inspire us. Without leadership a group of human beings quickly degenerates into argument and conflict, because we see things in different ways and lean toward different solutions. Leadership helps to point us in the same direction and harness our efforts jointly. Leadership is the ability to get other people to do something significant that they might not otherwise do. It's energizing people toward a goal.

Without followers, however, a leader isn't a leader, although followers may only come after a long wait. For example, during the 1930s Winston Churchill urged his fellow Englishmen to face the coming threat from Hitler's Germany. But most Englishmen preferred to believe that Hitler could be appeased—so that a war could be avoided. They were engaged in wishful thinking about the future and denial that the future would be dangerous. They resented Churchill for insisting that they must face the danger. They rejected his leadership. He had very few followers. But finally reality intruded—Germany went too far and war began. At this point Churchill was acclaimed for his foresight, and became prime minister of the United Kingdom during the Second World War. During this period almost all Englishmen accepted his leadership willingly.

True leadership is sometimes hard to distinguish from false leadership, which is merely a form of pretending. Winston Churchill was a real and great leader. But there are also people who wish to appear to be leaders, but aren't actually. They say that they are leading others; they posture as if they are setting direction and inspiring others. Yet often they are merely pretending. There's an old saying that the way to become a leader is to find a parade and run to the front of it. We refer to a person "leading" a parade, but walking at the front isn't really leadership unless the person in front is actually choosing the direction! If the person isn't choosing the direction, then being at the front of the line is merely a way to pretend to be a leader.

Leadership can be used for good or ill. Hitler seemed to be a leader of the German people, but he set an evil direction. He had great leadership skills, but put them to terrible uses. Sometimes people in business use leadership skills to exploit others. Sometimes people in charitable organizations use leadership skills to benefit themselves rather than the people they are supposed to help. Leadership skills can be perverted to pursue bad ends.

Without leadership, organizations move too slowly, stagnate, and lose their way. Much of the literature about organizations stresses decision-making and implies that if decision-making is timely, complete, and correct, then things will go well. Yet a decision by itself changes nothing. After a decision is made, an organization faces the problem of implementation—how to get things done in a timely and effective way.

Problems of implementation are really issues about how leaders influence behavior, change the course of events, and overcome resistance. Leadership is crucial in implementing decisions successfully.

Each of us recognizes the importance of leadership when we vote for our political leaders. We realize that it matters who is in office, so we participate in a contest, an election, to choose the best candidate. Investors recognize the importance of business leadership when they say that a good leader can make a success of a weak business plan, but that a poor leader can ruin even the best plan.

IMPORTANCE OF ETHICS

The danger that leadership will be perverted is why ethics are so important to good leadership. Ethics are the inner compass that directs a person toward what is right and fair. Only if a person has an inner ethical compass can he or she be sure that leadership qualities will not turn to evil ends.

WORK OF THE LEADER

Taking a leadership position means several things: A leader must have a vision of the future for the organization and its members.

Taking a Leadership Position

Taking a leadership position means:

- — Having a vision about what can be accomplished.
- — Making a commitment to the mission and to the people you lead.
- — Taking responsibility for the accomplishment of the mission and the welfare of those you lead.

— Assuming risk of loss and failure.

— Accepting recognition for success.

A leader must be able to express his or her vision clearly and in a compelling manner so that others are engaged by it.

A leader has to make a commitment to his or her vision, to the organization, and to the members of the organization. A leader can't be committed one day and uninterested the next. People will judge a leader by his or her commitment, and will commit themselves no more than the leader does.

A leader assumes a considerable amount of responsibility— not just for the mission that he or she urges others to accept, nor just for the organization he or she heads, but for his or her followers, their lives and efforts, as well.

A leader assumes risk. If there is no risk, little leadership is required. If the effort is easy and certain to succeed, anyone can, and probably will, "lead" it. But where the effort entails a risk of failure, then many people will quail before the challenge and leadership is necessary to get people to make the commitment and the effort to succeed.

In most organizations, one associates high levels of leadership with high levels of authority. The chief executive of a company usually plays more of a leadership role than people at lower levels of the hierarchy in the firm. It is the same in not-for-profits and government agencies. The higher on the job ladder a person is, the more she is expected to exhibit leadership.

In the military, however, the opposite holds true, and for a very good reason. In the military the greatest leadership challenge is to get other people to risk their lives in combat. Generally, the higher one goes in the chain of command, the less exposure he has to the battlefield, and the less exposure to men and women who are in combat.

The officers who have responsibility for commanding soldiers in combat have the greatest leadership challenge, for they must get others to risk their lives. An army sergeant major leading a deployment in Iraq in which he is responsible for more than 2,000 soldiers. Offered an opportunity to leave his assignment in combat, he chose to stay with his unit in harm's way. In so doing, he accepted one of the military's most significant leadership challenges.

The first responsibility in a position of leadership is to have a vision. The visionary leader must create his or her concept of what the organization can accomplish. A business leader may be leading a few people in a department or an entire company; a military leader a small squad or an entire army. The vision may be smaller when the group of people is small; and much broader when the group of people is large, but it must be forward-looking and exciting in either case.

VISIONARY LEADERSHIP

Visionary leadership requires:

- Creating a vision, a mission, and a strategy.
- Communicating the vision/mission/strategy and getting buy-in.
- Motivating action.
- Helping an organization grow, evolve, and adapt to changing circumstances.

The leader must also provide a mission—what needs to be done—and a strategy, a path, for how to accomplish the mission and achieve the vision, a way for the group to get there. But having an exciting vision, an exciting mission, and a careful strategy is not sufficient. A leader must clearly communicate them. Only if people grasp the vision can they commit to it, and buy-in is crucial to motivating action. Finally, a vision cannot be rigid and unchanging; it must adapt to changing circumstances, growing and evolving. Otherwise it becomes outdated and obsolete, and loses its power to excite and motivate people.

Leaders *versus* Administrators and Directors

Leadership is not the same thing as being in a position of authority. It is possible to be a boss in a company without being a leader. A boss can be more of an administrator than a leader.

Conversely, an administrator can be effective in his job without being a leader. The administrator is a bureaucrat— whether in government or in business—a person who keeps careful records and sees that things are done according to the rules. On the other hand, a leader can be effective without being an administrator—leaving rules, regulations, and their enforcement to others.

Administration is not as exciting a topic as leadership, but it is almost as important. The success of organizations depends to a great degree on how well they are administered. A director is often thought to be primarily an administrator. But a director is not an administrator; management requires a special set of skills of its own. And being a director is different from being a leader, as we shall see below. So there are three roles: administrator, director, and leader.

A director has the broadest role, and a good director has much of an administrator and a leader in him or her. A director needs to set direction and inspire others to get work done (leadership functions) and he or she needs to keep records and see that rules are followed (administrative functions).

The director is a necessary combination of leader and administrator. But leadership is the most important of the three roles.

Administrators

What does an administrator do? An administrator applies rules and regulations generally developed by top executives of an organization. He or she keeps records and fills out forms necessary to take administrative steps (like getting employees paid or reimbursing an employee for travel expenses).

ELEMENTS OF ADMINISTRATION

The elements of administration are:

- Making rules and regulations
- Making decisions that apply and interpret rules and regulations
- Keeping records
- Filling out forms

What does a director do?He or she makes plans and creates budgets that set forth in great detail how something will be accomplished and how much money and other resources (e.g., people, office space) are necessary to accomplish those plans and budgets. He decides who is going to be assigned to the necessary tasks and how they will fit into the organization. She supervises the actions people take, ensuring that they are doing the right things, that no money is being misappropriated or wasted (we call this "controlling"), and when problems arise she helps to resolve them. Finally, by combining these tasks into a coherent whole, the director makes the organization operate efficiently.

Running an organization effectively requires administration, management, and leadership. Leadership is ordinarily in shorter supply than administrative or managerial competence. Leadership is more important and more demanding for most people. Fewer people are able or willing to be leaders, so it tends to be a higher calling than administration or management.

There is a large literature discussing the differences between leaders and directors. There is also an important distinction to make between leaders and administrators. In general, a leader takes a broader view and points an organization toward necessary, even critical, change.

The core of the criticism in the literature is that organizations of all sorts (corporations, government agencies, and not-for-profit organizations) tend to be over-managed (and/or over-administrated) and under-led. Because of over-management and over-administration, organizations are slow to make necessary changes and achieve less than what they could. This is a substantial criticism that points to the importance of leadership.

The elements of management are:

— Planning and budgeting
— Setting direction
— Organizing and staffing
— Aligning the efforts of many people
— Controlling
— Decision-making and problem solving
— Motivating and inspiring people

NATURE OF LEADERSHIP

True leadership is special, subtle, and complex. Too often we confuse things like personal style and a position of authority with leadership.

- Leadership is not primarily a particular personality trait. A trait closely linked to leadership is charisma, but many people who have charisma (for example, movie actors and sports figures) are not leaders.
- Leadership is not primarily a set of important objectives. It involves getting things done.
- Leadership is not primarily a formal position. There have been great leaders who did not hold high positions—for example, Martin Luther King, Jr. and Jeanne d'Arc—and there are people who hold high positions who are not leaders at all, but administrators who don't want to rock the boat.
- Leadership is not primarily a set of behaviors. Many leadership manuals suggest that what defines leadership is things such as delegating and providing inspiration and vision; but people who are not leaders can do these things, and some effective leaders don't do them all.

Many discussions of leadership confuse any and all of the above— personality, important objectives, formal position, specific behaviors—with leadership. But leadership is more than any of the above characteristics. It's a process by which one influences the thoughts and behaviors of others in a substantial way. It may involve charisma, important objectives, a formal position, and a particular set of behaviors, but it is not limited to any of them. Because leaders can be so complex, we must be careful in our generalizations about leaders and their personalities. But not all leaders are such complex personalities, which is good for most of us who aspire to leadership.

SURROUND YOURSELF WITH QUALITY EMPLOYEES

The first rule of management is to surround yourself with

high quality employees. The talent level of your personnel will have a major impact on how successful you are as a director.

Directors must delegate tasks and responsibilities because one person can only do so much. The question is: to whom will you be delegating? Will you be delegating to someone who is hardworking or lazy, polite or rude, organized or unorganized, competent or inept? The answers to these questions will go a long way in determining how well you perform as a director.

The bottom line is that you had better surround yourself with talented people or you are not going to accomplish much. After all, how good would the greatest choreographer be if his dancers had two left feet? How good would the greatest football coach be if his quarterback couldn't throw, his receivers couldn't catch, and his offensive line couldn't block? How good would the greatest movie director be if he did not have great actors, great screenwriters, and great cinematographers?

In addition, synergy is created when a group of high quality employees work together. The standard of what is expected from each other is raised by subtle peer pressure. As a result, a culture of excellence is created and sustained. The problem is that the same thing happens on the flip side of the coin. High performing employees caught in a mediocre organization will adapt to their environment and become much less productive than they would have otherwise been under normal circumstances. So, what is it going to be: esprit de corps or esprit de bore?

"What if I can't afford to locate and hire high quality employees?" You might say "But the cost to land high quality employees can be high and I just can't afford to invest the time and money that it will take to obtain them." The truth is, you can't afford not to. For a product

to succeed, customers demand that it be consistently excellent. At the end of the day, the quality of your product is going to determine the success of your business, and your employees play a major role in determining that level of quality An ironclad principle of business is that if you tolerate mediocre employees, then you are tolerating giving your customers a mediocre product. Therefore, it is unacceptable to have an "OK" or "decent" or "so-so" group of employees unless you find it acceptable to give your customers an "OK" or "decent" or "so-so" product.

The extra cost and effort needed to lure a high quality employee to your company is actually little compared to all of the indirect expenses that will accrue as a result of having a mediocre employee. What is the cost if an employee can't get along with others? What is the cost if an employee doesn't show up to work on a consistent basis? What is the cost if an employee doesn't treat customers well? What is the cost if you have to correct his mistakes all the time? What is the cost if an employee quits soon after he is hired? Therefore, you can either invest a little more time and money now for a good employee or pay a lot later for a bad one.

"Where do I find high quality employees?" If you ever catch yourself saying "But I don't know where to find high quality employees," then it usually means that you are not trying hard enough. Don't just post a classified ad and see who comes knocking. *You must be as aggressive and persistent going after good employees as you are going after good customers.*

You should imitate the college coaches and recruiters who go after the best high school athletes. They are legendary in the techniques they use to lure the top talent to their schools. This is the mindset you must have when trying to acquire high quality employees. Figure out exactly what you want in an employee and then hunt that person down.Ultimately, though, your employees can be your best recruiters. If they are well paid, working with other good employees, being treated fairly and with respect, receiving appreciation for good work, having their ideas, opinions, and concerns heard, and working in a pleasant atmosphere, then they will spread the word about their experiences with the company. Soon, you will be flooded with job applicants. Remember, winners want to be surrounded by winners, and they want to play on a winning team.

When you hire an employee, you must figure out how well he will fit in with your other employees, because no employee works in a vacuum. Team chemistry is extremely important.

Because of the importance of team chemistry, your present employees should be involved in the interview process if they are going to be working with that person. For example, after you have interviewed the candidate, one of the employees could be assigned to show him around the company and introduce him to everybody. The employees could then have a group meeting with you and let you know what they thought about the candidate. You will then have more information upon which to make your final decision.

When employees are consulted, the selection goes from being "your" choice to being "our" choice. This consultation will make employees feel a much stronger bond to the team. They might even begin to take a more active role in trying to help locate high quality candidates.

❖❖❖

10

CHALLENGES OF DIRECTORS

The fragmentary reports from the world of directors often produce caricatures of the hardy types who reach for the general management rungs on the ladder. For example, the literature on management produces such widely held notions as these: that life gets less complicated as you reach the top of the pyramid. The director at that level knows everything that's going on in the organization, can command whatever resources he needs, and therefore can be more decisive. Another description pictures the general manager's day taken up with making broad policy decisions; a related version is that he spends most of his time formulating objectives. Still another identifies his primary activity as conceptualizing long range plans; or, in a large company, he may be seen meditating about the role of his organization in society.

Researching the management process when the director is aware that he is being studied sometimes produces strange results. Rarely is a good director able to think objectively about the management process as it is exemplified in his own methods.

You cannot expect a director to describe his methods even if he understands them. They border on manipulation, and the stigma associated with manipulation can be fatal. If ever the organization identifies you as a manipulator, your job becomes more difficult. No one willingly submits to manipulation, and those around you organize to protect themselves. And yet every good director is deep in this dilemma. Under competitive industry conditions, he is able to move his organization significantly toward the goals he has set, whether measured by higher return on investment, product improvement, development of management talent, faster growth in sales and earnings, or whatever.

Remember, this definition does not refer to the administrator whose principal role is to maintain the status quo in a company or in a department. Keeping the wheels turning in a direction already set is a relatively simple task compared to that of refereeing the introduction of a continuing flow of changes and innovations, and preventing the organization from flying apart under the pressure.

Considering this group of directors in action, on the job, what common characteristics do the successful ones exhibit? Do patterns seem to recur? Let us identify some skills or characteristics which are significant.

KEEPS INFORMED

A director should have a special talent for keeping himself informed about a wide range of operating decisions being made at different levels in the company. As he moves up the ladder, he develops a network of information sources in many different departments. He cultivates these sources and keeps them open no matter how high he rises in the organization. When the need arises, he bypasses the lines on the organization chart to seek more than one version of a situation.

In some instances, especially when they suspect he would not be in total agreement with their decision, his subordinates will elect to inform him in advance, before a decision is announced. In these circumstances, he is in a position to defer the decision, or redirect it, or even block any further action. On another kind of problem, the general director may learn after the fact that some decision has been made and implemented. The skilful director will ordinarily leave to members of his organization the judgement to decide at what stage they inform him.

Top level directors are frequently criticized by lower levels of management, writers, and consultants because after promotion they continue to enmesh themselves in operating problems rather than to withdraw to the "big picture." Without any doubt, some directors do get lost in a welter of detail. Not only do they dig into detail, but they insist that they make all the decisions. Superficially, the good director may seem to be caught in the same web, but his purposes are different. He knows that only by keeping well informed about the decisions being made can he avoid the sterility so often found in those who isolate themselves from operations. Many top executives who follow the advice to free themselves from operations soon find themselves subsisting on a diet of abstractions with the choice of what they eat in the hands of their subordinates.

As Kenneth Boulding puts it, "The very purpose of a hierarchy is to prevent information from reaching higher layers. It operates as an information filter, and there are little wastebaskets all along the way."

A real-life example which illustrates skilful management is that of one company president who sensed that his vice presidents were insulating him from some of the vital issues being discussed at lower levels. He accepted a proposal for a formal management development programme primarily because it afforded him an opportunity to discuss company problems with middle directors several layers removed from him in the organization. By meeting with small groups of these men in an academic setting, he learned much about their preoccupations, and also those of his vice presidents. And in this instance he accomplished his purposes without undermining line authority.

Certain directors seem to be able to respond almost immediately with a well-reasoned position on most of the problems and proposals coming to them. The explanation may rest not so much with a superior intellect as with a well-cultivated information network which gives an early warning and permits advance preparation.

The second characteristic or skill of the good director is an ability to save his energy and hours for those few particular issues, decisions or problems to which he should give his personal attention. There is a fine and subtle distinction between keeping fully informed about operating decisions and allowing the organization to force you into participating in them, or even worse, making them.

CHOOSING THE ISSUES

The good director knows that he can bring his special talents to bear on a limited number of matters. He therefore chooses those which he believes will have the greatest long-term impact and those where his own special talents can be most productive. Under ordinary circumstances he will limit himself to three or four major objectives during any single time period.

As he spots certain situations emerging from the organization, he will elect to become involved in the decision-making process. On the others, he will assure that the organization keeps him informed at various stages, but he will refrain from active participation. Unless this skill is exercised with great expertise, he may be accused of indifference to those issues which he keeps at arm's length. He trains his subordinates not to bring matters to him for decisions. The communication to him from below is essentially one of "here is our sizeup and here's what we propose to do."

The director is in a position to delay a course of action when he is informed prior to action, but in practice he seldom does hold up what his subordinates propose to do. His hearty encouragement is reserved for those projects which hold superior promise of a contribution to total corporate strategy. He simply acknowledges receipt of information on most matters. When he sees a problem where the organization needs his help, he finds ways to transmit his know-how short of giving orders, usually by asking perceptive questions.

POWER STRUCTURE

The third skill is the director's sensitivity to the power structure in the organization. In considering any one of the major and current proposals, he can plot the position of the various individuals and units in the organization on a scale ranging from complete, outspoken support down to determined, sometimes bitter and oftentimes well cloaked opposition. In the middle of the scale is an area of comparative indifference. Usually, several aspects of a proposal will fall into this area, and here is the area where the director can operate. He assesses the depth and nature of the blocs in the organization. His perception permits him to move through what is called as corridors of comparative indifference. He seldom challenges when a corridor is blocked, preferring to pause until it has opened up.

Related to this particular skill is the good director's recognition of the need for a few trial balloon launchers in the organization. He knows that the organization will tolerate only a certain number of proposals which emanate from the apex of the pyramid. No matter how sorely he may be tempted to stimulate the organization with a flow of his own ideas, he recognizes the advantages of cultivating trial balloon launchers or idea men in different parts of the organization. As he studies the reactions of key individuals and groups to the balloons these men send up, he is able to make a better assessment of how to limit the emasculation of the various proposals.

Seldom, too, does he find a proposal which is supported by all quarters of the organization. The emergence of strong support in certain quarters is almost certain to evoke strong opposition in others.

Consider this example of a vice president who for some time had been convinced that his company lacked a sense of direction and needed a formal long-range planning activity to fill the void. Up to now, his soft overtures to top management had been rebuffed. And then, he spotted an opening.

A management development committee had proposed a series of weekend meetings for second-level officers in the company. After extensive debate, but for reasons not announced, the president rejected this proposal. The members of the management development committee openly resented what seemed to them an arbitrary rejection. The vice president, sensing a tense situation, suggested that the same officers who were to have attended the weekend management development seminars be organized into a long-range planning committee. The timing of his suggestion was perfect. The president, looking for a bone to toss the committee, acquiesced immediately, and the management development committee in its next meeting enthusiastically endorsed the idea.

This vice president had been conducting a kind of continuing market research to discover how to sell his long-range planning proposal. His previous probes of the "market" had told him that the president's earlier rejections of his proposals were not so final as to preclude an eventual shift in the corridors. He caught the committee in a similar conciliatory mood and his proposal rode through with colours flying.

As a good director stands at a point in time, he can identify a set of goals, albeit the outline may be pretty hazy at times. His timetable, which is also pretty hazy, suggests that some must be accomplished sooner than others; and that some may be safely postponed for several months or years. But at this point the director has a still hazier notion of how he can reach these goals. He assesses key individuals and groups. He knows that each has its own set of goals, some of which he understands rather thoroughly, others which he can only speculate about. He knows also that these individuals and groups represent blocks to certain programmes or projects and that these points of opposition must be taken into account. As the day-today operating decisions are made, and as proposals are responded to both by individuals and groups, the director perceives more clearly where the corridors of comparative indifference are.

AVOIDING SPECIFICS

The fourth skill is the ability of the director to satisfy the organization that it has a sense of direction, but without ever getting himself committed publicly to a specific set of objectives. This is not to say that the good director does not have objectives, both personal and corporate, long term and short term. They are significant guides to his thinking, and he modifies them continually as he better understands the resources he is working with, the competition, and the changing market demands.

But as the organization clamours for statement of objectives, these are samples of what they get back:

"Our company aims to be number one in its industry"

"Our objective is growth with profit"

"We seek the maximum return on investment"

"Management's goal is to meet its responsibilities to stockholders, employees and the public."

Statements such as these provide almost no guidance to the various levels of management, and yet they are quite readily accepted as objectives by large numbers of intelligent people.

Why does the good director shy away from precise statements of his objectives for the organization? There are many good reasons for not being more precise. The main reason is that he finds it impossible to set down specific objectives which will be relevant for any reasonable period into the future. Conditions in business change continually and rapidly, and corporate strategy must be revised to take the changes into account. The more definite the statement of strategy for the organization, the more difficult it becomes to persuade the organization to turn to different goals. Even if management were capable of this kind of master planning, before it could get the objectives comprehended by the organization, the targets would have shifted.

The public and the stockholders must perceive the organization as having a well-defined set of objectives and a clear sense of direction. But in reality the good top director is seldom so certain of the direction in which he should take the organization. Better than anyone else, he senses the many, many threats to his company, threats which lie in the economy, the actions of competitors, and not least within his own organization. Better than anyone else, too, he knows that he is continually on the tenterhooks of whether to pause and re-evaluate or to forge ahead.

COMMUNICATION BY CONSISTENCY

The skilful director also knows that objectives are impossible to state clearly enough so that everyone in the organization understands what they mean. They get communicated only over time by a consistency or pattern in operating decisions. In instances where precise objectives are spelled out, the organization interprets them so they fit its own needs.

The subordinates who keep pressing for more precise objectives are in truth working against their own best interests. Each time the objectives are stated more specifically, the subordinate's range of possibilities for operating is reduced. The narrower field means less room to roam and to accommodate the flow of ideas coming up from his part of the organization.

The good director's reluctance extends into the area of policy decisions. He seldom makes a forthright statement of policy. Some executives spend more time in arbitrating disputes caused by stated policies than in moving the company forward. The management textbooks contend that well-defined policies are the sine qua non of a well-managed company.

The president of one company deliberately leaves the assignments of his top officers vague and refuses to define policies for them. He passes out new assignments with seemingly no pattern in mind and consciously sets up competitive ventures among his subordinates. His methods, though they would never be sanctioned by a classical organization planner, are deliberate and, incidentally, quite effective.

EVOLVING POLICIES

Since good directors don't make policy decisions, does this mean that well-managed companies operate without policies? Certainly not, but the policies are those which evolve over time from an indescribable mix of operating decisions. From any single operating decision might have come a very minor dimension of the policy as the organization now understands it. It's the patterns as they emerge from a series of decisions which set up guidelines for various levels of the organization.

The skillful director resists the urge to write a company creed or to compile a policy manual. Preoccupation with detailed statements of corporate objectives and departmental goals, comprehensive organization charts and job descriptions-this is often the first symptom of an organization in the early stages of atrophy.

The "management by objectives" school, so widely heralded in recent years, suggests that detailed objectives be spelled out at all levels in the organization. This method is feasible at lower levels of management, but it becomes unworkable at the upper levels. In his own mind, the good top director must think out objectives in detail, but ordinarily some of the objectives must be withheld, or at least communicated to the organization in modest doses. A conditioning process, which may stretch over months or years, is necessary in order to prepare the organization for radical departures from what it is already striving to attain.

Take, for example, the president who is convinced that his company must phase out of the principal business it has been in for thirty-five years. Although this has become one of his objectives, he cannot disclose it even to his vice presidents, whose total know-how is in the present business. A blunt announcement that the company was changing horses would be too great a shock for most of them to bear. And so he begins moving toward the objective of altering the existing business, but without a disclosure to his management group.

If the director attempts to spell out his objectives in detail, a task which is almost impossible to accomplish, perhaps his major accomplishment will be to complicate the task of reaching those objectives. Specific, detailed objectives simply give the opposition an opportunity to organize its defenses.

And now we come to the fifth and most important skill, the ability to discern opportunities and relationships in the stream of operating decisions which flow past the general director each day. In reviewing the activities of the organization, he suggests modest alterations which move the organization in small increments toward the goals he has set. He understands the concept of marginal increments which was introduced to business management by the economist. He recognizes the futility of trying to push total packages or programs through the organization. He is willing to take less than total acceptance in order to achieve modest progress toward his goals.

PIECING PARTICLES

The good director then, avoiding debates on principles, tries to piece together particles, which may appear to be incidentals, into a program which moves at least partially toward his objectives. His attitude is based upon optimism and persistence. Over and over, he says to himself, "there must be some parts of this proposal on which we can capitalize."

Whenever the director identifies relationships among the different proposals before him, he knows that they present opportunities for combination and restructuring.

It follows that the good director is a man of wide ranging interests and curiosities. The more things he knows about, the more opportunities he will have to discover parts which are related. This process does not require great intellectual brilliance or unusual creativity. The wider ranging his interests, the more likely he will be able to tie together several unrelated proposals. He is skilled as an analyst, but even more talented as a conceptualizer.

If the director has built a solid organization, it will be difficult for him to come up with an idea which no one in the organization has ever thought of before. His most significant contribution may be that he can see relationships which no one else has seen.

Take this example of a division director who had set as one of his objectives, at the start of a year, an improvement in product quality. At the end of the year, in reviewing his progress toward this objective, he could identify three significant events which had brought about a perceptible improvement.

Early in the year, the head of the quality control group, a long-service director who was doing only an adequate job, asked for assignment to a new research group. Opportunity number one permitted the division director to install a promising young engineer in this key spot.

A few months later, opportunity number two came along. The personnel department proposed a continuous programme of checking the effectiveness of training methods for new employees. The proposal was acceptable to the manufacturing group. The division director's only contribution was to suggest that the programme should include a heavy emphasis on the employee's attitude toward quality.

A third opportunity came along when one of the division's best customers discovered that the wrong material had been used for a large lot of parts. The heat generated by this complaint made it possible to institute a completely new system of procedures for inspecting and testing raw materials.

As the division director reviewed the year's progress on product quality, these were the three most important developments. None of them could have been predicted at the start of the year, but the division director was quick to see the potential in each as it popped up in the day-to-day operating routines.

CHANGE IS ESSENTIAL

The good director can function effectively only in an environment of continual change. A cartoonist in Saturday Review has caught the idea as he pictures an executive seated at a massive desk instructing his secretary to "send in a deal. I feel like wheelin'." Only with many changes in the works can the director discover new combinations of opportunities and open up new corridors of comparative indifference. His stimulation to creativity comes from trying to make something useful of the proposal or idea in front of him. He will make strategic change a way of life in the organization and continually review the strategy even though current results are good.

Charles Lindblom has written an article with an engaging title "The Science of Muddling Through." In this paper he describes what he calls "the rational comprehensive method" of decision-making. The essence of this method is that the decision-maker, for each of his problems, proceeds deliberately and one step at a time to collect complete data, to analyze the data thoroughly, to study a wide range of alternatives, each with its own risks and consequences, and finally to formulate a detailed course of action.

Lind-blom immediately dismisses "the rational comprehensive method" in favour of what he calls "successive limited comparisons." He sees the decision-maker as comparing the alternatives which are open to him to see which most closely meets the objectives he has in mind. Since this is not so much a rational process as an opportunistic one, he sees the director as a muddler, but a muddler with a purpose.

Ansoff in his book on corporate strategy espouses a similar notion as he describes what he calls the "cascade approach." In his view, possible decision rules are formulated in gross terms and are successively refined through several stages as the emergence of a solution proceeds. This process gives the appearance of solving the problem several times over, but with successively more precise results.

Both of these authors are moving us closer to an understanding of how directors really think. The process is not highly abstract, as a director searches for means of drawing into a pattern the thousands of incidents which make up the day-to-day life of a growing company.

The general director is sitting in the midst of a continuous stream of operating problems. His organization presents him with a flow of proposals to deal with the problems. Some of the proposals are contained in voluminous, well-documented, formal reports; some are as fleeting as the walk-in visit from a subordinate whose latest inspiration came during the morning's coffee break. Feeling no compulsion to classify his problems, he knows how meaningless it is to say, "This is a finance problem, or that is a communications problem." He is, in fact, undismayed by a problem that defies classification. As the late Gary Steiner put it, "he has a high tolerance for ambiguity."

In considering each proposal, the general director tests it against at least three criteria: First, will the total proposal, or more often will some part of the proposal, move the organization toward the objectives he has in mind? Second, how will the whole or parts of the proposal be received by the various groups and subgroups in the organization? Where will the strongest opposition come from, which group will furnish the strongest support, and which will be neutral or indifferent? Third, how does the proposal relate to programs already in process or currently proposed? Can some parts of the proposal now in front of him be added on to a programme already under way or can they be combined with all or parts of other proposals in a package which can be steered through the organization?

SEARCH FOR OPPORTUNITIES

Reviewing briefly the five skills of the general director:

— *Skill One:* Keeping open many pipelines of information. No one will quarrel with the desirability of an early warning system which provides varied viewpoints on an issue. The difficulty comes in that very few directors know how to practice this skill, and the books on management add precious little to our understanding of the techniques which make it practicable.

— *Skill Two:* Concentrating on a limited number of significant issues. No matter how skilful the director is in concentrating his energies and talents, he is inevitably caught up in a number of inconsequential duties. Active leadership of an organization demands a high level of personal involvement, and personal involvement brings with it many time-consuming activities which have an infinitesimal impact on corporate strategy.

- *Skill Three:* Identifying the corridors of comparative indifference. Are there inferences here that the good director has no ideas of his own, stands by until his organization proposes solutions, that he never uses his authority to force a proposal through the organization? Such inferences are not intended. The key message is that a good organization will tolerate only so much direction from the top; the good director therefore is adept at sensing how hard he can push.
- *Skill Four:* Giving the organization a sense of direction with open-ended objectives.
- *Skill Five:* Spotting opportunities and relationships in the stream of operating problems and decisions.

FRUSTRATION FOR PLANNERS

Interestingly, professional planners may be irritated by a good general director. Perhaps in this paper they can find a partial explanation for their frustrations. Most of them complain about the lack of vision of top manage-ment. The planners devise a master plan, but the president seems to ignore it, or to give it minimum acknowledg-ment by borrowing bits and pieces for implementation.

Many planners seem to think that they need only to draw up a master plan and present it to top management, and its power will be obvious to everyone and its implementation automatic. The general management level executive, however, knows that even if the plan is sound and imaginative, the job is only begun. The long, painful task of implementation will depend upon his skill, not that of the planner.

In conclusion, if this analysis of how skilful general directors think and operate has validity, then it is of significance for several groups in business as well as for educators who are training men and women for management.

The investment community is giving increasing attention to sizing up the management of a company being appraised. Thus far, the analysts rely mainly on results or performance rather than on a probe of management skills. Current performance can be affected by many variables, both favourable and unfavourable, and is a dangerous base for predicting what the management of a company will produce in the future. Testing the key directors of a company against the five skills holds promise for evaluating the caliber of a management group.

In today's frenzy of acquisitions and mergers, why does a management usually prefer to acquire a company rather than to develop a new product and build an organization to make and sell it? One of the reasons can be found in the way a general director thinks and operates. He finds it difficult to sit and speculate theoretically into the future as he and his subordinates fashion a plan to exploit a new product. He is much more at home in taking over a going concern, even though he anticipates he will inherit many things he doesn't want. In the day-to-day operation of a going concern, he finds the milieu to manoeuvre and conceptualize.

Both the director who is building his own company and the man who is moving up through the hierarchy of a larger organization require essentially the same capabilities for success. The five skills are fundamental to the director with commitment in either situation.

Scarcely any director in any business can escape the acutely painful responsibility to identify men with potential for growth in management and to devise methods for developing them for broader responsibilities. Few line directors or staff professionals have genuine confidence in the yardsticks and devices they use now. The five skills offer possibilities for raising an additional set of questions about management appraisal methods, job rotation practices, on-the-job development assignments, and the curricula of formal in-house management development programmes.

One group of distinguished executives ignores with alarming regularity the implications of the five skills. These are the presidents of multi-division companies who promote successful division directors to the parent company level as staff officers. These "promotions" frequently put line directors on the sidelines and out of the game for the rest of their careers.

ACHIEVING A STRETCH GOAL

The organization you're managing is responsible for something—whether it's performing a business process, supporting some other organization, developing a new product, or getting new customers. There are goals associated with your objectives, and if your organization is aggressive then those goals require more than the typical amount of effort. It's going to take some careful planning for you to figure out how to apply your organization's people and resources to achieve an aggressive goal. You're going to have to motivate people, remove roadblocks from their path, and focus them on the things that are most important. It's a stretch goal, but you can achieve it—maybe even surpass it.

BRINGING OUT THE BEST IN YOUR EMPLOYEES

All employees have good days and bad days. Some of the causes are out of your control. But it's important that you take steps to make as many days as possible "good days." Here are some of the things that you can do:

- Treat every employee with respect. If you have praise for the employee, give the praise in front of coworkers. If you have criticism for the employee, give it in private. For all but the worst underperforming employees, make sure that the praise happens much more often than the criticism.
- Help employees align their personal goals with their work goals. Talk with each employee about his or her personal goals: what they want to get out of life, where they want their career to go. To the extent possible, use this information to help you allocate work assignments.
- Provide a work environment that is appropriate for the work and conducive to employee well-being. A comfortable work environment makes your employees more productive.
- Encourage employee communication and cooperation.

DEALING WITH UNDERPERFORMING EMPLOYEES

Not all of your employees will do their best. Some will have personal issues that interfere with their work. Technically it's not your problem, but in reality any issue that contributes to an underperforming employee is your problem. You'll help employees cope with personal issues, you'll provide motivation and counsel, maybe steer them to appropriate resources inside or outside your company. You'll "carry" your underperforming employees to a point, and then beyond that point you'll have to ease them out of your organization. You'll be humane, but you have to balance the needs of the organization with the needs of the employees.

DEALING WITH OUTSTANDING EMPLOYEES

Some of your employees obviously outperform the

others. That's good news for your organization, but it presents its own set of challenges. Outstanding employees need special treatment. You want them to keep doing an exceptional job but that usually means that you'll have to pay them special attention. They need recognition for their talents and efforts. They need encouragement, training and guidance. And above all they need to know that they have a career path in your company, even if that career path takes them out of your organization.

You'll be tempted to hold on to your outstanding employees and keep them from being promoted out of your organization. You shouldn't do that. When an employee star outgrows your organization, the best thing for your company is to make sure that the employee finds a home in another part of your company where he or she can continue to contribute. And ultimately, you'll be rewarded for your good deed of helping the employee achieve his or her potential. Your reputation as a "team player" and good manager will grow, and your own career will be enhanced.

❖❖❖

SELECTED READINGS

Anand, V.; Rosen, C. C. "The Ethics of Organizational Secrets". *Journal of Management Inquiry* 17 (2): 97. 2008.

"Basic Role of the Board". Governance Basics. Institute on Governance (Canada). Archived from the original on 2007-12-30. Retrieved 2008-01-27.

Buckingham, Marcus, and Clifton, Donald. *Now, Discover Your Strengths.* New York: Simon & Schuster, 2001.

Buckingham, Marcus, and Coffman, Curt. *First, Break All the Rules: What the World's Greatest Managers Do Differently.* New York: Simon & Schuster, 2001.

Cai, J., J. L. Garner, and R. A. Walkling, Electing Directors. *Journal of Finance* 64 (5), 2387–2419. 2009.

Capstone Publishing *The Capstone Encyclopaedia of Business.* Oxford, U.K.: Capstone Publishing. pp. 79-80. 2003.

Charles Handy. *21 Ideas for Managers: Practical Wisdom for Managing Your Company and Yourself,* First ed. San Francisco: Jossey-Bass, 2000.

Charles W. L. Hill, and Gareth R. Jones, Strategic Management. Houghton Mifflin. 2001.

Chhaochharia V, Grinstein Y. Corporate governance and firm value: The impact of the 2002 governance rules. *The Journal of Finance.* 2007.

Covey, Stephen M. R. *The Speed of Trust: The One Thing That Changes Everything.* New York: Free Press, 2006.

Craig S, Lattman P. Companies May Fail, but Directors Are in Demand. *New York Times.* 2010.

Eugene H. Fram with Vicki Brown, *Policy vs. Paper Clips: Selling the Corporate Model to Your Nonprofit Board,* 2nd Edition, Families International, Milwaukee, WI. 1995.

Hewlett, Roderic. *The Cognitive leader*. Rowman & Littlefield Pub Inc. 2006.

Hopt, K.J. 'The German Two-Tier Board: Experience, Theories, Reforms' in KJ Hopt and others. (eds), *Comparative Corporate Governance: The State of the Art and Emerging Research*. Clarendon 1998.

Kraakman, Reinier H.; et al. *Anatomy of Corporate Law: A Comparative and Functional Approach*. New York: Oxford University Press. 2004.

Lencioni, Patrick. *The Five Dysfunctions of a Team*. San Francisco: Jossey-Bass, 2002.

Lowry, John; Dignam, Alan. *Company Law*. New York: Oxford University Press. 2006.

Maxwell, John. *Leadership 101: What Every Leader Needs to Know*. Nashville, TN: Thomas Nelson, 2002.

McNamara, Carter. "Overview of Roles and Responsibilities of Corporate Board of Directors". *Free Management Library*. Authenticity Consulting, LLC. Retrieved 2008-01-26.

Neff, Thomas, and James Citrin. *You're in Charge: Now What?* New York: Crown Publishing, 2005.

Robert III, Henry M.; William J. Evans, Daniel H. Honemann, Thomas J. Balch. *Robert's Rules of Order Newly Revised*. Cambridge, MA: Da Capo Press. 2000.

Samson, D., Daft, R. *Management*. Second Pacific Rim edition. Melbourne, Victoria: Thomson, 2005.

Shivdasani A, Yermack D. CEO involvement in the selection of new board members: An empirical analysis. *Journal of Finance*. 1999.

Wagner, Rodd, and James K. Harter. *12: The Elements of Great Managing*. Princeton, NJ: Gallup Press, 2006.

Watkins, Michael. *The First 90 Days: Critical Success Strategies for New Leaders at All Levels*. Boston: Harvard Business School Publishing, 2002.